Keeping Couples in Treatment

Library of Object Relations
Series Editor: David E. Scharff and Jill Savege Scharff

The Library of Object Relations provides an expanding body of theory for understanding individual development and pathology, human interaction, and new avenues of treatment. They apply to realms of experience from the internal world of the individual to the human community, from the clinical situation to everyday life, and from individual psychoanalysis and psychotherapy, to group therapy, couple and family therapy, and to social policy.

Keeping Couples in Treatment

Working from Surface to Depth

Carl Bagnini

JASON ARONSON
Lanham • Boulder • New York • Toronto • Plymouth, UK

Published by Jason Aronson
A wholly owned subsidiary of The Rowman & Littlefield Publishing Group, Inc.
4501 Forbes Boulevard, Suite 200, Lanham, Maryland 20706
www.rowman.com

10 Thornbury Road, Plymouth PL6 7PP, United Kingdom

British Library Cataloguing in Publication Information Available

Library of Congress Cataloging-in-Publication Data

Bagnini, Carl, 1941-
Keeping couples in treatment : working from surface to depth / Carl Bagnini.
p. cm.
Includes bibliographical references and index.
ISBN 978-0-7657-0903-5 (cloth : alk. paper) -- ISBN 978-0-7657-0904-2 (electronic)
1. Couples therapy. 2. Marital psychotherapy. I. Title.
RC488.5B324 2012
616.89'1562--dc23
2012012123

♾️™ The paper used in this publication meets the minimum requirements of American
National Standard for Information Sciences Permanence of Paper for Printed Library
Materials, ANSI/NISO Z39.48-1992.

Printed in the United States of America

For Susan, Jenna, Brian, Karen, Barry, Connor, Basie, Luke, and Evan.

Your love is the grounding in my life.

Contents

Preface

Keeping Couples in Treatment: Working from Surface to Depth

Carl Bagnini, LCSW, BCD

In the more than forty years of working in the trenches, I have run the gamut of couples I believed could not or would not remain in treatment. The immediacy of couple behavior is endlessly fascinating, and therapists falter under its emotional weight. When disturbed couples arrive at our offices, partner's agendas are in conflict. Couples are a complex mixture of two personalities. Thinking about couples reminds me of succotash; corn and lima beans have distinct flavors but when cooked together a new distinctive flavor emerges from the merger of the two personalities (Scharff and Bagnini, 2001). The therapist has to (1) be alert for couples who rigidly retain their distinct uniqueness at the sacrifice of blending into something mutually enhancing, and (2) recognize the opposite type—those that seek merger into an undifferentiated "we-ness." Overly close couples keep the therapist at bay by self-protecting. The partners feel lost without their adhesive (symbiotic) bond because having separate identities triggers an unconscious terror of falling apart. These are but two examples of hard-to-reach couples. Treatment couples can range from unstable and chaotic to coherent and colonized. Each couple's particular attachment style heightens frustrations for a therapist lacking a theory to explain the unconscious matrix of pathological partnerships.

In my early career my piecemeal approach was woefully inadequate and couples would take over me. It took years of study, self-reflection, and wisdom from talented mentors, and many hours with couples, while researching couple therapy literature, to *provide grounding in an approach that would not sacrifice the personality of each partner or the couple system of two intrapsychically connected human beings.* Finding an in-depth clinical approach to couples is difficult for therapists because psychoanalytic understanding of couples as a small group is sparse in the couple psychotherapy literature, and psychoanalytic institutes focus on individual treatment. Within the couple therapy literature, writings that discuss in-depth work with couples are in the minority. Keeping in mind that psychoanalytic approaches to couple therapy are underrepresented in training, we wish to close the gap, and in the following chapters we draw from robust clinical ideas that (while not widely disseminated) are time tested in treatment. This book was written to bring the special dynamics of couples and couple treatment to the reader in a digestible way.

We need a thinking bridge that navigates the couple's troubled waters, and organizes the therapist's psychological experience. The object relations theory I have adapted in this book opens our eyes to couple unconscious mental and affective process and guides clinical decisions. A flexible method is offered that explores varieties of couple psychopathology at a deeper level than other couple therapy approaches. The clinical material is organized by a conceptual map of two individuals in an intimate relationship. As we will see, the nature of coupleness presses into our psyches and soma, causing internal reactions that differ in magnitude and complexity from individual therapies. What makes couple therapy different is the triangular treatment system consisting of the couple and ourselves.

The three-person system is the clinical system. The interactivity is difficult to capture in a larger system than in a dyad but we strive to comprehend its complexity to derive the benefits.

The couple conceptualization of two individuals and their relationship is derived from the pluralism in clinical psychoanalysis (Scharff and Scharff, 2011, p. 4) that embodies a two-person psychology. We start with the individual unconscious and expand our clinical conceptualization to the interpersonal sphere. Constructing a theory for couple practice has led to my appreciation of two vertices of an intimate partnership and a paradox of couple life: (1) the inherent tensions that interplay between two individual's needs and (2) the requirements of being in an emotional partnership.

The clinical and theoretical material in this book was written for the beginning couple therapist, the seasoned individual therapist who wants to transition to couple therapy, and experienced couple therapists wanting exposure to in-depth contemporary psychoanalytic practice with hard-to-reach couples. The book offers guidance acquired from my turbulent initiation into couple therapy, guidance that can detoxify emotional reactivity and retain the therapist's "desire" to be of help. I write from the perspective of a working therapist; not too top heavy with theory but offering sufficient conceptual guidelines that explain the clinical encounter.

A treatment approach needs theory that contrasts ordinary couple development with the dynamics of disturbed relating. Explanatory concepts about unconscious communications within intimate adult relationships are needed scaffolding for relevant treatment. We use ideas about unconscious transmissions of dangerous desires, flawed development, and unfinished childhood business. We gather knowledge of two complex individuals and their development to understand why and how each chose a particular other as solution, or search strategy, to avoid or end prior suffering from unmet intimacy needs. However, for the therapist without comprehension of unconscious process, keeping individuals *and* the couple relationship in mind may not be possible. Careful assessment that favors theories of unconscious communication promotes a sensitive and sensible working partnership. We note that the therapist must accept and contend with anxiety, anger, and fear associated with unmet or underrepresented needs for marital bonding that permeates the treatment for some time.

As we move through the various chapters, the reader will observe significant challenges await the therapist who views the couple and each partner with equal consideration. I am often persuaded by a positive or negative identification with one partner to forgo my *couple-think,* and take as fact one partner's view of the *real* truth about couple life. As we will see partners can be persuasive, if not demanding, when seeking the therapist as "judge" of who is at fault for partnership discord.

Becoming an effective couple therapist means being able to stay on task. We will define the task of couple therapy and determine the "how" of staying with it. Oscillations between self and other are the couple's basic modus-operandi and their fluctuations pressure us to remain steady while being pushed in alternating directions. In individual analytic therapy, we search for truth, but with couples we deal with separate agendas in the context of a relationship. Theory is a range finder that helps us prevent side-taking by providing a conceptual map of the deeper basis for a couple's rigidified differences. We need a theory that explains the individual, dyad and larger system to make sense of the lopsidedness of three in the setting. We include the therapist in the treatment because he is part of the dynamic system of interaction. The idea of a triad therefore involves thinking about everyone's mental space.

Mental space is the psychological container and flow chart for individual psychic structure, and in the clinical situation, interpersonal interactions activate the individual's psychic experiences in projected forms as partners seek a host for their unmet needs. The unprocessed past is existentially revealed in the treatment setting by the interactions of the couple with the therapist. Simply put, interpersonal interactions are surface representations of unconscious objects occupying each partner's mental space. Because one's internal objects are in conflict with the reality (limitations) of an external world, each partner's distorted perceptions threaten their partner's view. A vicious cycle of rigid beliefs and unmet needs easily takes over the interpersonal mental space.

We need concepts to dynamically understand the high levels of emotional discharge of couples in treatment. Developmental deficits and frustrated needs challenge the coping capacity of a partnership. Phantasies about not feeling loved, hateful feelings, and frustrated longings are affectively represented when couples interact. Mental space is where self and other meets.

In my view mental space adds much to our practice theory, as it offers a conceptual map that morphs troubling couple interactions. In describing the functions of mental space, we develop a mentalizing capacity, leading to a practical language for deconstructing the couple's exchanges. The utility of mental space keeps us from succumbing to the ordinary tipping when partners hotly insist on one version of couple reality. From the vantage point of mental space, its usefulness carries with it not so much a proper instruction but a provocation (Fisher, 2005) that shakes up the ordinary and reaches for a dystonic realignment that the couple can tolerate for the sake of new knowing. In short, our interpretive capacity is most beneficial when reframing surface discharges by in-depth references in which raising traumatic history speaks to modify "madness." Interpretive comments based on the therapist's empathic curiosity are "meaning-making" or symbolizing experiences.

A case example to illustrate: Jeff (31) and Sonya (28) are cohabitating in Jeff's house and are engaged to be married. They are in couple treatment to address fighting that alienates them for days at a time; the fights start over where the dog should sleep at night, which family to visit on weekends, and Jeff's involvement in business, which Sonya feels forces her to be on her own. In a recent session (number 13), they got into a heated re-argument that started during the Christmas/Hanukkah holiday break of ten days. Sonya wanted to light the eighth and final candle of a menorah, which Jeff strenuously objected to, as she is not Jewish. In the session, the couple was quite caught up in their fight and was looking over to be sure I was paying attention. My role was limited to attentive listener. I silently picked up where the anger was most potent—Jeff's fury over Sonya's insisting that he was not really Jewish but "American," while he was insisting he was Jewish. Sonya could not therefore understand why Jeff excluded her from lighting the last candle, especially being that she had bought him the menorah. She accused Jeff of marginalizing her with statements like: "You are not part of the 'inner'" group. Sonya rebutted: "Neither are you and you do this at other times." The fighting words escalated the couple into a projective "gridlock" (Morgan, 1995).

My take on the exchange was that each was feeling persecuted and was persecuting in return due to not recognizing the underlying feelings of exclusion. Anger ruled and covered over the hurt because neither partner realized they were hurt. In my countertransference I felt persecuted and marginalized by the couple and thought it related to the underbelly (unconscious basis) of the aggression. Realizing my countertransference and knowing their ancestry and family backgrounds, I now had something in mind to offer. I told them it was my turn to say something and asked if either had suffered discrimination in early life. A light went off. They each told a story, calmly and poignantly. Sonya was beaten up by Jewish kids as a youngster because she was Catholic; Jeff was beaten and bullied by Irish kids because he proudly admitted he was Jewish, not thinking there was anything wrong with that. Sonya went on about how simply being female in this world meant being marginalized. I had their attention, as their mental space had shifted from a form of mutual "madness" to historicizing their relational conflict. I pointed out that in the fighting they were repeating what was done to them with each other, marginalizing each other but also attacking the persecutor from whom no one protected them as young children. They listened and went on fighting, albeit less passionately. Change takes time, especially when there is evidence of long-term splitting between despair in early holding deficits and rage (in reactions to being excluded). In chapter 4 we discuss splitting.

This vignette brings alive our theory in use when working in depth. Mental space is applied to the relationship to determine how containment functions in the group. The map entails several levels of attention to couple process, but these levels are not intended as orderly steps. We observe interpersonal interactions (surface communications, including angry discharges), imagining what the interpsychic issues are (what is common to couple suffering as a shared experience but split off from awareness), and we consider each partner's intrapsychic issues, defenses, and coping strategies during stressful sessions. We note the interpenetration of individual object relations in the couple's interactions and their effects on therapist mental space. Depending on what resonates with the therapist, countertransference awareness aids the assessment process by revealing new material to explore. Engaging the clinical field in an orderly manner is impossible due to the amount of data and oscillating emotions occurring in any one session. Each therapist will determine—based on comfort, experience, unconscious vulnerability and preference—how much attention is given to the various dynamics within the field of mental space.

The realignment I am seeking in learning the art of couple therapy includes therapists' personal reactions to their couples. A shake-up (dystonic) accompanies learning when recognizing that cognitive knowledge is insufficient for working in depth; to arrive at affective attunement, we have to be disturbed. I share aspects of my personal experience with the reader when couples get me to become emotionally involved and occasionally trapped. The personal material in the chapters invites the reader to become more self-revealing in thinking about the personal self and "clinical" self as essential variables in the "how" and "why" of couple practice.

Countertransference enables the tracking of our reactions to couple projections. Countertransference is broadly conceived here as the therapist's unconscious benign to distorted personal tendencies, some of which lead to inevitable enactments (conflicted situations) which move the treatment in various directions; we react when affected by dystonic emotional experiences. Countertransference is stimulated by unconscious process; as such it ebbs and flows, it is impossible to plan for, it helps us reach an intimacy with the couple not accomplished by other means, and (by its unique nature as unconscious communication) it cannot be mastered. When we freely associate and try it out it is a splendid companion and clinical guide.

From many couple assessments we have learned what each partner contributes to the relationship, though it may appear that only one partner carries the hurt and the other the victimizer role. Like the couple, we too can become trapped by a powerful bias over whose unmet needs and anxieties truly matter. That is what couples initially present—a "me versus you" litany of grievances. Underlying dyadic longings, losses and angers about injustices are sent and received within the couple relationship and may parallel the therapist's personal history with marital or other intimate relationships.

A good-enough therapy has to access the above dynamics in an even-handed approach. Therapist self-awareness melds with analytic availability and mobilizes the desire to focus on an aspect of couple history, helping to formulate working hypotheses. The vulnerable self of the therapist becomes the template for locating couple unconscious process. This book brings together the dynamics occurring within the treatment system that are neglected by more limited approaches that conceptualize only the couple or only the partners as separate individuals. This approach is comprehensive and includes the therapist's personality and vulnerabilities. This approach also helps prevent couples from leaving prematurely and helps the therapist refrain from taking sides. We strive for sensitivity to each partner's contribution. Increased self-awareness, as noted, prevents splitting the couple, and considering that we are psychologically conditioned by our primary mother-child dyad, we remain open to the couple relationship and embrace being in a triangle, which can come more natural as we examine the pull in us to be drawn to only one spouse or the other.

A central motive for writing this book concerns reports that graduate and postgraduate training gives insufficient attention to the challenge of keeping couples in treatment. For the one-on-one therapist motivated to start couple work, few training options are available. We will address elsewhere the paucity of training opportunities in couple and family treatment compared with training programs in individual therapy. There are many obstacles to being prepared for couples. Getting one's feet wet without drowning when inviting both partners into the consulting room invites trepidations that force therapists to give up on learning the craft. This book encourages therapists to persevere with couples by bringing the reader into the consulting room, in an up-close glimpse of couple-therapist interactions, learning as we go through some challenging cases.

Several causes of premature termination come to mind: There might be a lack of fit between a therapist's personality and a particular couple that results in their dropping out abruptly. However, I suspect that an early dropout is often due to the therapist's tendency to lose empathy through faulty containment (also described as reverie or affective attunement) of the couple and reverting to a one-on-one individual focus. Insecurity about managing couple situations results in feeling that couple therapy presents an overwhelming task. From the couple's point of view, the therapist can be viewed as taking sides. Mistakes in couple work stem from limitations in emotional stamina triggered by varieties of couple anxieties and defenses that prevent the therapist from mentalizing the psychological field. Couple-therapist interactions require empathic curiosity that fosters a working bond essential to keeping couples involved. As you can see, therapist anxieties are part of the picture.

Bader and Pearson (2011) concluded that one-on-one therapy is preferred even though neuroscience shows that we are relationally prewired. Yet, therapists are reluctant to take up couple therapy due to fears of the emotional turmoil associated with having troubled couples in the consulting room. The authors underscore the fears of seeing couples but do not take up the requisite knowledge and training that can prepare therapists wanting to learn this modality. They do caution that individual therapy can be hazardous to a marriage because it is too safe a haven from revealing selfishness and deception in the spouse being treated. In my experience, the concern about collusive pairing in one-on-one treatment is somewhat valid. Well-trained couple therapists that do one-on-one treatment keep a more balanced view about collusive transference-countertransference when their theory informs them about compensatory pairings associated with idealized therapy transferences. The split between the *understanding* therapist versus the *never understanding* spouse is an ordinary hazard when working with a relationship problem with only one partner in the room. Seduction in the transference presses the therapist to take *my side*. The therapist must understand the personality dynamics of a troubled patient who wants the therapist to be everything the at-home partner is not. The patient's couple relationship is transferred onto the dyadic therapy, and the therapy "pair" replicates the disturbed marriage with its unprocessed childhood issues.

Thus far we have begun theorizing about the couple as a complex small group, featured the treatment unit as a triad, discussed mental space, and identified ordinary therapist anxieties. These are key practice elements developed and illustrated in the book. The book's focus on unconscious dynamics of the couple and the therapist is the basis for depth work. We also want to support therapist growth. To accomplish the task of describing couple-therapist dynamics, the cases in the book were written in an interactive process form so the reader can follow shifting dynamics in couple-therapist communications. In reading the cases, we may renew couple therapist's faith that they can learn to keep couples in treatment. We want to counter the loss of morale and to bridge the gap between the desire to help and learning how to make a difference.

THE ORIGINS OF THE PRACTICE THEORY IN THE BOOK

The first book that uniquely featured in-depth, theory-based, case-centered treatment for couples was the 1991 book, *Object Relations Couple Therapy* by David E. Scharff and Jill S. Scharff, two psychoanalysts trained at the Tavistock Clinic in Great Britain. The present book builds on their rich clinical ideas that were introduced in the United States almost twenty years ago. Among the few books that feature psychoanalytic approaches to the couple, are: *Repairing Intimacy* (Siegel, 1992), *Psychotherapy with Couples* (Ruszczynski, 1993), *Intrusiveness and Intimacy in the Couple* (Ruszczynski and Fisher, 1995), and *Treating Borderline States in Marriage* (McCormack, 2000). I have met wonderful thinkers overseas and borrowed from their ideas concerning couple dynamics. I rely on many core concepts associated with the faculty at the Tavistock Centre for Couple Relations. Mary Morgan (1995, "The Projective Gridlock"), Warren Colman (1993, "Marriage as a Psychological

Container"), Chris Clulow (2006, *Couple Psychotherapy and At-tachment Theory*), and Ronald Britton (1990, *The Oedipus Complex Today*) stand out.

This book is partly a result of the few contributions just cited. I have added recent theoretical developments and applied them to my clinical experience. Each therapist develops a unique style of work, so I expect readers to compare the clinical representations of what I was thinking at the time, in moment to moment responses, to what they might have thought or done differently.

Psychoanalytically trained therapists are familiar with unconscious process, but those new to couple work naturally focus on the individual psyche due to insufficient expansion of theory into the mental space of the triad (Suttie, 1935). Therapists that believe the couple is merely two individuals are limited to treating one individual at a time in the same therapy. They inevitably leave out important interpersonal-interpsychic dimensions of a unique group (Scharff and Scharff, 2011). Whether in the field a long time or newly graduated, they may enter couple practice lacking training about the treatment field of two spouses, their relationship, *and* the therapist. Therapists report the press of triadic mental space but remain stuck in an *I-thou* dichotomy; one result of inadequate conceptualizations is persuading couples to behave in accordance with or to submit to doctrinaire methods. Regardless of a therapist's training, without a theory expansion sessions may be spent micromanaging couple anxieties. Therapists may be unable to conceive ways to deal with unmanageable couple anxieties because their own anxieties run so high.

The material in the following chapters provides the necessary theory for practice that can help the reader learn to decipher the couple domain and supply containment for a variety of treatment cases. The book is couple centered, focusing on an object relations approach to working in depth with troubled couples, and it features ways to keep difficult couples in treatment when less sophisticated methods fail to do so. It explores situations in which the therapist faces warring partners and finds a way to be of use. Warring couples increase the possibility of taking sides, splitting the couple into two cases, or losing them in an affective flood.

Therapists get scared both when things become heated and when the couple withdraws into a freeze-up. For the beginning couple therapist, the book offers a rationale for treatment and offers technical improvements from individual therapy to bear on work with couples. I value self-reflection in assessment and give examples of my personal reactions throughout the treatment cases. Moving from case to case the reader will note the emotional and mental flexibility necessary to avoid putting couples into categories that lead to mistakes. The book guides the inexperienced therapist through the pain, rage, and attacks on the frame when in deeply distressing situations. For the experienced therapist, the book emphasizes the couple as an interpsychic system best treated using an in-depth understanding of intrapsychic-interpsychic communications. The cases represent a variety of problems difficult to treat at any level of therapist experience.

The practice approach to contemporary object relations couple therapy is a thoughtful, patient, and creative endeavor. It features a reflective approach individualizing each couple. The chapters favor a person-in-relationship centered focus over popular "problem-solving" approaches that prescribe advice through therapist-centered dominance. The book explores difficult couple situations and clinical interventions that demonstrate a capacity to engage, which experienced therapists will find liberating. I have come to appreciate how the complexity of couple treatment is better understood when utilizing contemporary knowledge of triadic mental space.

The introductory chapter sets the stage for presenting the surface-to-depth approach to couple therapy. I introduce the reader to my evolution and heritage underpinning my view of couple practice. I explain the origins of the book and compare my approach with other couple treatment methods. Unconscious couple process is identified as the focal point for learning in depth work. Chapter 2 is a personal story describing my realization of the fall-out and pressures of being a psychoanalytic couple therapist. In chapter 3, object relations couple therapy comes alive in a case study and session transcripts. Chapter 4 expands the practice approach by presenting three marital types encountered in couple practice. The clinical approach is adapted to each of the three couples who present particular developmental deficits and pathological fits. Chapter 5 addresses narcissistic personalities in marriage. I describe severe pathological states in couples with narcissistic transferences and discuss safeguards for retaining clinical capability. The case material in chapter 5 presents how narcissistic pathology over-determines mate selection. We provide a lens for sensitive work with traumatized patients and their mates who paradoxically use the mind of the therapist to repeat past suffering and helplessness, while seeking a different outcome.

Unconscious issues that lead to infidelity and divorce (chapters 6 and 8) are grounded in practice experience with couples who seek treatment in the throes of marital breakdown. Chapter 6 presents couples undergoing a traumatic breakdown with volatile outcomes (affairs). A complex clinical case of infidelity details countertransference, when at first treating one partner and then the couple. The clinical material demonstrates reworking the past and grieving losses.

A few words are in order to set the stage for cases of infidelity. Practical approaches suggest forgiveness for infidelity. Though often recommended by self-help literature, it has a forced quality to it, as though time-lived experiences must be speedily replaced by enforced optimism, referred to as "moving on." Unconscious time is not temporal time, and mistrust, deception, and secrets described in chapter 6 have a longer shelf life than the affairs. Instead, I show how the couple needs time to revisit old wounds to gradually recover. Chapter 7 presents couple dreams as a neglected topic, beginning with an essay on dreams and moving into the ways couple dreams inform treatment. Divorce (chapter 8) is discussed from the therapist's position; in cases where separation or divorce may be an unanticipated therapy outcome, therapists need a theory to help them maintain a balanced view on the limits of therapy intended to save a marriage. In the divorce chapter, I address the therapist's suffering and ways of maintaining coherence and emotional resilience. Chapter 9 describes a unique case in which the author's capacity for containment was compromised until his dream helped to salvage the situation. Chapter 10 explores the growth of the couple therapist in light of the evolving requisites for effective therapy developed in the book; use of self and creativity are integrative for working from surface to depth. The treatment triad is further elaborated in chapter 10. Chapter 11 reviews the aims of the book, and we assess the usefulness of this method of treatment. In this final chapter, we wonder if our destination was reached in terms of the clinical pathway we traveled. Detailed attention is given to therapists' personal feelings and style, which enable them to hone a capacity to deal with difficult couples. The final chapter discusses termination.

The writing of this book has been influenced by a small and sturdy group of psychoanalytic searchers, mentors, and colleagues. When presenting in the United States and internationally, I have been in the company of major contributors to the field of psychoanalytic couple therapy. Whether in formal meetings or in leisurely social venues we compare and critique techniques and theory in current practice. Teaching and supervising alongside my esteemed colleagues at the International Psychotherapy Institute (IPI) in Washington, D.C., in Europe and in Panama has been a rich source of inspiration. Jill S. Scharff and David E. Scharff, former codirectors and senior colleagues at IPI, have been at various times my coauthors, editors, mentors, program collaborators, teachers, and supporters of many creative and mutual efforts on behalf of children, couples, families, and object relations education. I cannot say enough about their individual and collective influences on my growth as an analytic therapist, writer, theorist and presenter. For nineteen years, they have been generous with their time, by helping me organize fragmented ideas, while providing encouragement and inspiration. I have written papers, articles, and book chapters as a lead author and as coauthor with Jill Scharff, and David Scharff is the motivator for this book. They are a consistent source of synthesis and expansion (Scharff and Scharff, 2011), which fuels my thinking in the field of object relations and related theories and practice, for which I am most grateful.

I have collaborated with friends and colleagues at IPI who live and work in the United States and Panama. They are a source of personal growth and love of our profession. My wife, Susan, a gerontologist and clinical social worker, and I have spent many winters in Florida with Stan Tsigounis and Hilary Hall. While teaching their lively group of local students, and enjoying the welcome contrast with New York weather, the social camaraderie and stimulation of many talks about our cases is always beneficial. Sharon and Doug Dennett, Judy and Bob Rovner, Charles Ashbach, and Walton Erhardt have been bed-and-breakfast buddies at the Rovner's D.C. digs over the years during IPI conference weekends and week-long training programs. The time we spend is a source of deep clinical thinking, and during breaks from serious theorizing a near riot of belly laughing and good cheer balances out the workload.

The life of a clinician can be isolating, and we need resources and support for continued learning. I have been a long-term group member of Charles Ashbach's Bion telephone seminar, which continuously re-thinks the writings of Bion and other psychoanalytic thinkers. Within the safety of the group, we often question what we think we know about unconscious process and the ways suffering and sacrifice in our roles as healers require ongoing discussion and rediscovery of our own narcissistic motives.

Mike Stadter and Jane Prelinger are dear Washington friends and colleagues with whom I have co-chaired and co-led small groups. They always offer refreshing commentary on featured guest presenters and grounding with family stories. My Panama friends and colleagues, Yolanda Varela, Lea De Setton, and Vali Maduro, among many others, are sources of cross-cultural application of object relations clinical theory. I have learned much from my Panamanian experience, which reinforces the importance of multicultural sensitivity. Their hospitality is also unmatched. We have taught, co-chaired conferences, and co-led affective groups together and their humanity and clinical sensibilities inform and enrich me. I apologize for the limitations of space and omitting other colleagues and students at IPI who have shaped my clinical mind and touched my life.

I have taught alongside and created curricula and new programs with colleagues from university postgraduate clinical programs in psychoanalysis and clinical social work. They have influenced my clinical thinking and provided me opportunities to bring my clinical approaches to their respective training programs. I deeply appreciate Dr. Art Mones, former Director of the St. Johns University Postdoctoral Program in Couple and Family Therapy in Queens, NY; Dr. Michael Zentman, Director of the Adelphi Derner Postgraduate Program in Couple and Marital Therapy, on Long Island, NY; Dr. Judith Siegel, Program Director of the NYU Post-Masters Certificate Program in Child and Family Therapy in Manhattan; and Dr. Phyllis Cohen, Director of the New York Institute for Psychotherapy Training. These colleagues have developed training programs of cutting-edge integrative clinical approaches grounded in psychoanalytic thinking. I appreciate the enrichment that our associations have provided and the continued growth that comes from working closely with new groups of students seeking quality training provided in their venues.

To my patients, past and present, I owe the greatest debt. Some of those I worked with early in my career more or less suffered for my newness and naïveté. I learned from them what it is like to want to make a difference, but I was often too zealous. From my unstable beginnings, I learned to be patient while suffering inner and outer pressures to offer concrete advice before I knew enough to decide a proper response. Later, my obsessive search for a good-enough theory placed patients in conflict with my internalized mentors, supervisors, and the printed word. My need at that time was for certainty, resulting in an approach that was too structured, and at times I was too rigid when applying the analytic frame.

Over time I have clinically matured so that the patients I see today have inherited the benefits of my prior successes and failures. My current couples benefit from a more seasoned and scarred veteran's vantage point. So a fond thank you to my patients, past and present, for teaching me humility over hubris. There is no easy route to becoming a skilled therapist, and my patients have been the most reliable, ongoing source of learning how to do effective couple work, and in many instances I have been forgiven for treatment errors.

The editors and staff at Jason Aronson and Lexington Books deserve recognition and appreciation for organizing my efforts and assisting in the publication of the book. Lindsey Porambo and Amy King in editorial acquisitions were patient and professionally astute. They enabled me to stay on track, and to keep my voice authentic throughout the chapters. I thank them for ensuring the book's coherence.

Chapter One

Introduction

In this book, I discuss in-depth couple therapy and present clinical approaches derived from understanding what lies beneath the torment that brings wounded couples into treatment. The most complete source of clinical information about couples is the archive of their lived experiences. Ambiguities abound in conflicted couples, involving unconscious motives and unknown anxieties in addition to the presented problems at intake. The couples described in the following chapters cannot tolerate closeness, yet demand it and repress feelings while forcing their partner to expose feelings in their stead. No cookie-cutter approach is offered with difficult couples, as each treatment situation is unique and requires a sufficiently courageous therapist to remain open to tracking unconscious processes. To keep these couples in treatment, we have to journey beyond the obvious anger and disorganizing conflicts to explore ways to make meaningful contact with the frightening dimensions of the couples' confused identities and broken dreams.

This book examines the clinical experience of doing in-depth work from a psychoanalytic object relations perspective; it draws from British and American object relations theories, applied to the field of couple therapy, and features the therapist's thoughts through self-reflection and emotional resonance. By detailed case reporting, I identify theory in action and bring the reader close to the therapist's subjective responses as he or she engages the couple in the setting, and, most importantly presents the therapeutic results. The surface-to-depth approach has us consider the forest *and* the trees of the couples' relationships. Transference and counter-transference are examined as technical tools and building blocks for effective therapy. The reader is placed in the position of learning about working in depth in a thoughtful way with the couple in mind. Each chapter draws the reader into difficult treatment situations with a variety of couple types that illustrate technical considerations applied to the unique personalities and conflictual circumstances of each couple.

"Keeping couples in treatment" builds on many years of clinical practice with children, adolescents, couples, and families and immersion in group affective learning (Scharff and Scharff, 2000). Each chapter reproduces in-depth clinical practice with couples drawn from many cases. The object relations concepts I apply to couple treatment come from individual, family, and group psychoanalytic traditions, expanded and adapted to couples. I present clinical experience with a variety of couples and situations; they represent an ordinary grouping of my daily work. In my case reports, I tackle universal problems and challenges to clinical efficacy that have been underrepresented in the couple therapy literature. Working with couples is a challenge that, for the most part, is not taught in training institutes or psychotherapy programs.

The dearth of training leaves beginning therapists and seasoned therapists looking for help with too few opportunities to receive it. Most psychotherapy training focuses on one individual at a time; this focus places couples and their prospective therapists in a bind in which the requisite knowledge and skill sets for working in a triad (a gestalt—the sum being greater than the individual parts) are woefully unavailable. Therapists take on couples anyway and take their chances. Although I would agree that each couple we take on has its own trajectory of emotional and mental distress and is looking for a proper fit with a therapist, this book avoids the willy-nilly one-size-fits-all approach, as well as the purely courageous approach (blindly following one's intuition/impulses, or "wild analysis").

EVOLUTION OF A PSYCHOANALYTIC OBJECT RELATIONS COUPLE THERAPIST

In writing this book, I became aware of deficits and feelings of incompetence in my early training when failing to keep couples in treatment. My intent here is to give an account of what I have culled from my clinical evolution. I became interested in object relations couple therapy in 1986 and discovered two important clinical truths. First, the object relations method provides comprehensive understanding of couples inside and out. However, another important lesson to be learned involves couple and therapist vulnerability. My object relations training is an open-systems therapeutic model that views vulnerability as an asset for building therapeutic capability, not a shaming secret to be avoided. Therapist vulnerability must not be repressed but rather must be constantly scrutinized for the treasures that stir within our wounded selves. Seeking experience that contributes to clinical understanding is a head, heart and body exposure to traumatic process that accompanies many couples to our offices. After emotion-laden sessions we are left with more of the couple in us than they have received from us. Our containment (remaining steady and available) is easily overtaken by the couple's disturbances.

Working with couples and training couple therapists interested in gaining mastery in the modality came later in my clinical evolution. When looking back, I have little doubt that my parents' turbulent marriage, ambivalent sibling relations, developmental strivings, and blind spots produced an intense motive to make a better life. I owe a great deal to my analyst, who was good company on my journey to make a difference. Surely the reader is aware that there is a motive that underlies our choice of profession, stemming from the wish to rescue others in our families of origin to heal ourselves, and we suffer for it. Therapist suffering varies depending on the intensity of our unmetabolized mission to heal parts of ourselves over and over again with each new case. But not to worry; learning is painful. To deny that fact is to lose opportunities to rework our object relations and improve competence. When embracing that reality, we are in a position to feel closer to our patients as we get stung by their pain—deficits, terror, and rage rank high among unmetabolized turmoil that brings patients in, and these emotions stir our personal wounds. In a sense, we and the couple are striving to reduce heavy lifting by turning old baggage, which represents unmetabolized conflicts, into luggage, representing improved choices about what to pack and unpack with insight.

I came to couple therapy last in learning the major clinical modalities, starting with young children in play therapy, moving into latency and adolescent group work with urban youth, then family treatment, and lastly the couple relationship. Couple therapy eventually became a major specialty. My practice is currently 60 to 70 percent couple work. Individual psychoanalytic therapy is the grounding for studying and learning about the treatment dyad in depth; however, I was always drawn to the triad.

I was and am still drawn as the oedipal child to be curious about the amazing varieties of intimacy longings in primary pairings. Oedipal issues do not disappear; they resurface throughout life, modified by our attention to feelings of inclusion and exclusion in work and personal relationships. Couples follow suit with similar feelings of exclusion, or of becoming too intertwined with a partner. We pay attention to many reiterations of dyadic and triadic tensions or conflicts. Everyone wants to be the special child, and being thrown out of Eden is due to pursuing knowledge about the union of male and female (the Tree of Life), a subject of interest in every clinical situation in which human beings are seeking oneness with another while retaining cohesion as a separate self. There is family competition, between siblings and parents, that is normal, but in pathological situations the distress reaches crippling proportions. Rejection, neglect, and lack of attunement are common in disorganized and traumatized families. Unhealthy regard for self and other is eventually revealed by slavish or tyrannical behaviors. In this sense, history becomes destiny for making an unhealthy choice of a marital partner.

Personal sharing is partly narcissistic, but our unconscious motives and strivings are always involved when moving from surface to depth. There is no shortcut concerning this issue of how the personal influences the clinical, and vice versa. As I think about couple work, I also think about the growth of the therapist. Neither the couple nor we can circumvent the gooeyness of the unconscious world; we have to go through it—only long-cuts are allowed when working in and with depth. This book counters the tendency to split the couple into two cases at the first sign of troubled relating and to seek a shortcut by working with each as an individual. I hope to assist therapists to choose another direction to slow down and hold the triadic frame and assisting the couple to stay together in treatment.

A note on the political-economic climate and couple psychotherapy training: Coming from a minority position, I am hoping the reader will pardon this short diversion tying the lack of comprehensive couple and family psychotherapy training in the United States to the historical overemphasis on the individual.

We have elsewhere pointed to the few books and papers written from a psychoanalytic perspective on couple therapy. Political economics and social policy shape governmental programs established to address couple and family mental health. The culture of individualism trickles down to practitioner's choices of training in psychotherapy. Millions are invested in pharmacology advertising that insists there are medicines for all human suffering and that therapists should readily resort to them. One psychotherapy training consequence of viewing human suffering purely from an individual biological/medication perspective is increased behavioral and short-term "how to" treatments, thereby reducing consumer's choices and availability of psychodynamic/systemic and humanistic therapies. Ever notice the result when a suffering individual takes the advertised medication? We see only the positive outcome, although the doctor/actor rushes manically through an incredible list of side effects, including suicide. What happens to the marriage when the sick person feels better? In some cases, when one spouse improves, the other becomes stricken, or a child becomes symptomatic. In my early training we called this dynamic "family scapegoating," in which the family unconsciously "needs" one member to carry the "sickness" of the unit. When an index member improved with treatment other members acted out or broke down.

Couple and family therapists are a group capable of intervening with a wide range of populations, but we are small in numbers. We observe increases in breakdowns within family and couple life. The economic cost alone of family breakdown is in the billions: divorce, health problems, cost of two residences, incarceration, crime, delinquency, and stresses on young children, to name a few. The prevailing climate in mental health funding ignores couple and family therapy. The public in need of specialized care is underserved. Mental health services fail to serve troubled relationships, and we see the increased trend in medicating. This is true in both publicly funded mental health programs and fee-for-service private practice. This reality is not a good selling point for the insurance industry entrusted to provide mental health coverage, public or private.

In addition, couple therapy is not recognized by the insurance industry as a mental health treatment modality and is not listed in insurance reimbursement codes, whereas family therapy is reimbursable. This gap forces some therapists to dance around who is the patient in the couple, opting for an individual diagnosis to justify couple treatment, or they opt for family therapy which is clinically inaccurate and potentially unethical. Therapists electing to steer clear of the insurance bind cannot help patients with reimbursement, which forces out-of-pocket sacrifices for the consumer who needs marital or intimate partnership help. The couple or their employers are purchasing outpatient mental health coverage they cannot utilize.

Another pressure on clinicians joins the insurance debacle in psychotherapy reimbursement with the recent controversy over the new (DSM-5). A blog article (in www.Newsworks.org) written in December 2011 was distributed to members of Division 39, Section VIII of the American Psychological Association (couple and family psychoanalysis) by the chair of the APA Committee on Public Policy and Liaison (Cindy Baum-Baicker). The proposed new manual instigates an alarming trend in American psychiatry (Baum-Baicker, 2011). In the listserv e-mail, Baum-Baicker states, "As we have loosened the criteria for psychiatric illness (DSM's 1–4) we have simultaneously grown the number of psychiatric disorders [by] 108 percent." She points to diagnostic "inflation" and the increased advertising of psychopharmacology, especially with children and the elderly, as the result of a shift away from clinician input into the DSM-5 toward reliance on researchers.

To add injury to insult, training institutes are increasingly pressured to shorten postgraduate psychotherapy programs. Economics and competition for students in some instances reduces standards in favor of learning more quickly. My observation is that learning psychotherapy cannot be rushed; rushing leads to insufficient training and incomplete treatments. Less time to learn couple therapy fosters inadequate shorter-term treatments driven by manic over-zealousness. The therapist cannot make meaningful contact with the couple's internal conflicts. Underprepared therapists too quickly utilize surface and behavioral approaches that are technique driven. I believe the focus on mobilizing the couples by technical maneuvers is insufficient for many complex marital dilemmas and for resolving the multiple levels of trauma that many couples bring.

To summarize, the current alarming movement in expanding the number of mental disorders and the political economics of the mental health industry can only be touched on here—increasing psychiatric diagnostics, shorter time to learn psychotherapy, media blitzing of psychotropic medications, underfunding of mental health programs, and confused insurance reimbursement policies. Many mental health organizations and professional groups are rallying against these trends. We need to get out of our offices and join with others interested in promoting adequate training and public access to in-depth psychotherapy.

Note that our nonpsychodynamic training culture and political climate are driven by the pragmatic, from surface to surface—accomplish more for less with directive interventions and therapist-centered tactics disguised as technically valid and evidence-based shenanigans, with little clinical regard for the internal world of relationships. Within the paucity of couple training available, the movement is toward interactive relational approaches that assume that all clinical work should be focused on correcting the here-and-now couple relationship, and an idea is permeating with some relational folks that we should be suspicious of delving too much into unconscious motives and the distant past. I suspect a zealous embrace has taken hold in the belief that what goes on in the here and now between partners and with their therapists is sufficient to guide most interventions.

Transference from this viewpoint is limited to therapist-couple interactions, without regard for a rich psychoanalytic heritage that can add necessary depth and directionality for elaborating more complex historical derivatives of transference issues. Some therapists prefer to believe that the past is always accessible in the present, so they mentalize their cases accordingly (nonjudgmental focus on the here-and-now experience of the couple). The present is also in the past and there is richness and dimensionality of transferences that are clinically revealing and affectively useful. For example, couples who bear witness to each other's developmentally centered crises often report reduced judging, improved empathy, and a release of embarrassment or shame for previously held childhood blame associated with overwhelming events—for example, in a heartfelt release from lifelong blame for the sudden death of a parent following an argument.

Aspects of Imago therapy concern me. When supervising imago-trained couple therapists, I have observed that the approach can be zealous and naïve. I do not admire training that focuses excessively on changing couple interactions by directive means and to insist on a structural change in relating. Couples from this standpoint must be compliant, or they will fail. One couple who could not process hateful feelings had an imago therapist that insisted they say only positive things to each other. This may be one outrageous example of a therapist's doctrinaire approach, but there are many other examples of pushing couples to comply with a set of techniques within a short time. To be sure, there are situations in which couples may benefit from therapist-centered or doctrinaire approaches that emphasize active behavioral recommendations, homework assignments, and so forth. Does implementing this directive approach imply that there are no other options? Once directive means fail to accomplish a stated goal, what comes next? And what of the transference when a couple fails to please their therapist?

As the reader can see, I have strong reactions to overreliance on directive methods in psychotherapy, but I am especially concerned about the current state of couple practices because, as I have been reporting, couple therapy is more demanding on the emotional resilience and tolerance of the therapist. A premise of this book is that unprepared therapists lose themselves in the affective turmoil of couples and may resort to institutionally sanctioned behavioral methods to survive by taking charge. Defensive uses of techniques and overtly directive methods can be reaction formations designed to sooth the therapist's ruptured ego. I have observed many instances of resorting to manic activity from my years of supervising.

I am interested in preserving a deep clinical heritage and philosophy that views marriage as an intimate and special unconscious two-person field that is embedded in cultural prescriptions and thwarted development. Treatment addresses conflicted psychic worlds that produce projective processes between the partners that operate at the center of marital longings and conflict. These internal worlds invoke competing ancestral expectations and conflicting objects that need to be translated and empathized with; they lie beneath the surface, as does an iceberg mostly remain out of our sight. We know what can happen when an ocean liner miscalculates the actual size of an iceberg in its path. The couple heading for an iceberg may temporarily need a therapist's firm hand, but steering requires awareness of the depth, circumference, distance and thickness of the mass, not to mention its familiarity to the couple; sometimes icebergs are constructed by a couple needing an external obstacle to avoid contact with an internal obstruction.

What happens to partners in the throes of current conflicts who carry stored up emotionally preformed conflicted internalized self parts, good and bad? For therapists limited to problem-solving techniques, what happens after the couple cannot solve their problems? Are they shamed or encouraged to try the same concrete operations over again? In the author's experience, the technical assistance provided in popular couple therapy literature is suitable for a limited couple population: cooperative, neurotic, capable of feeling regret, seeking responsible behavior, and trusting authority figures (experts).

I have provided case material and conceptual explanations of a powerful model of treatment designed especially for difficult couples. The couples described in the book remained in therapy from six months to six years. I believe the couples stayed in treatment because they came to trust the therapist, the therapeutic approach, and a transforming experience. As the chapters unfold, notice the limitations of each couple. What is their level of trust in each other and in the therapist from the start? What are the levels of stuckness, emotional turbulence, or reticence? How disturbed are they, and in what areas? The mode of therapy used in this book was established to comprehend difficult couples and personalities, and although no single therapy model succeeds in every case, I illustrate what can be done under conditions of maximum holding and containment in the setting. The next chapter paints a picture of the author's unexpected rediscovery of what lies beneath during a recreational hike in the woods, with reference to the importance of containment and its pressures on the couple therapist. As we will discover, a psychoanalytic way of working influences the therapist's core psychological makeup due to the required self-examination of unconscious process.

Chapter Two

A Walk in the Woods

From Surface to Depth

One early spring day, my young grandsons and I were enjoying a walk through the nature preserve by my house, a grassy eastern prairie with a still unblemished topography. As we walked they stooped to look intently at twigs, examined leftover fall leaves, and explore more closely under rocks and logs in search of bugs, snails, or whatever else might be emerging after winter's hush on visible life. Being the grownup on the other hand, I, as my taller self implies, attended to the aboveness around us: the tall trees, some plump and turning green, others gaunt with broken limbs. And looking higher, I studied the color and formation of clouds while a red hawk hovered and scanned the prairie below, I deduced, in search of food. These sites captured my gaze in contrast with my lower-to-the-ground grandboys, who possessed the curiosity and detective prowess of young explorers. As we progressed along the path, my attention shifted from high to low, now taken up with the various reactions going on around me. Each of the children spoke proudly and emotively of their findings and questioned each other and me as to what each discovery meant to them; we discussed how new growth and decay were symbiotically connected to change.

Later I recognized the symbolism and hidden wisdom of the paradox I had been exposed to during the treasured moments with the boys. They looked for what was deep, beneath the surface of things (which was obvious given their stature, levels of development, and tactile-sensory comprehension), while I was preoccupied with the aboveground world. I further reflected on the juxtaposition: was I taking depth for granted, and was I under an illusion from my training and clinical experience that had assumed the world beneath was sufficiently internalized? And did I, therefore, place it out of sight, whereas for the boys, each discovered living and decaying organism had its connection to what came before, evoked by the wonder of new experience? Why in a setting that provided the obvious and the yet-to-be-discovered (surface and depth) would I have opted for the former?

I believe couple therapy training in the current culture fosters a surface and directive technical approach. I suspect my head in the air and my preference for surface material on the nature walk had stemmed from the tendency to avoid the deeper aspects of comprehending nature in depth. My weekend break from couple work momentarily produced avoidance, a common defensive response to engaging in emotionally charged work. The sojourn into nature probably signaled the usual suffering I experience when being close to the emotional turbulence of couple process. As a result, I distanced myself from my usual interest in what lies beneath (whether nature or human nature). I suspect that my week's work with many couples was too disturbingly near and I took a surface route on my journey as a kind of preservationist time out. Such is the toll taken of the couple therapist who invests in the emotional life of the couple, and for whom surface and depth are both the canvas and template that provide a more complete cornucopia of needed colors, textures, and images. This illustrates my style of couple work. Learning about the world of couple experience from this perspective offers the therapist clinical depth and breadth to guide therapeutic encounters.

I suspect that whatever theory of couples and couple therapy one follows, an important motive (conscious or unconscious) is selecting a useful set of tools and perspectives with which to do thoughtful work. A theory prepares the therapist to select among the many dimensions of couple interactions, patterns, and behaviors to encounter; theory can also distance us from the internal catastrophe of the couple because theory is cognitive, whereas experiential work is emotional and psychosomatic (viz., a body-mind oscillation of the primitive-sensorial, the felt, and the thought-and-not-easily-remembered versions of couple experience). The emotional world of couple strife is what we address. We need a treatment theory that preserves a measure of internal coherence in doing the work while recognizing the levels and types of emotional distress that will break us down. I engage with the couple in locating catastrophes in the service of understanding. I search for hope that the couple may survive and potentially come alive as we locate psychic and interpersonal pain. At the same time, I internally cringe when affected by the slings and arrows hurled back and forth, and at me, during dramatic expressions when love seems buried by hate.

EXPLAINING THE INTERPLAY BETWEEN SURFACE AND DEPTH

This book is an attempt to reveal and define the practice of couple therapy from the perspective of object relations theory and practice. Why do we work from a surface-to-depth paradigm? Couple therapy begins with the couple and includes the therapist at the point of initial contact. The field of the couple is characterized as two individuals, their personalities, intergenerational baggage, and strengths. We look at the current life course and marital backgrounds, and we study typical couple approaches to work, family, and love relations informed by goals, beliefs, and attitudes toward handling life's problems, traumas, and deficits. The surface of the couple relationship is relevant because the couple persona draws on strengths and deficits in the to-and-fro of average conscious and habitual expectations and co-influences in the course of the marriage.

The surface of couple therapy deals with the conscious communications, habits, and purposeful influences on couple and family life, as explained by the couple from the outset and throughout the course of sessions. The surface content includes accompanying behavior, psychosocial functioning, health circumstances, and conscious communication and is the portion of the field that establishes the couple's view of their situation. *Surface* refers to the observable presented by the obvious, the topography of he said and she said, he did and she did, and the resulting conflicts pressed by unresolved differences. Working in depth applies to the archeological dig beneath the ordinary that transforms the conscious communication of the couple to an unconscious level of comprehension. The goal is to locate the couple's unconscious dynamic history after tapping into the limits of conscious communications that usually repeat the obvious without leading anywhere; when a level of new experience occurs, connections/linkages release frozen effect or explain confused or driven effect. A case example illustrates the surface dimension.

Mary and Bob are in their second marriage of twenty years. In the initial session, they mentioned their twenty-one-year-old daughter from the current marriage, Mary's two sons from the prior marriage in their thirties (from whom she is estranged), and Bob's son who died in infancy from leukemia. Their daughter is attending college; she was conceived when they were dating. They married two years later after Bob decided it was time to be a family; Mary told him that he did not have to marry her. From the start, Mary said the couple therapy was her last stop, as she seriously wanted to end the marriage. She was the reason they were there; for years Bob had thwarted attempts at going for help. Bob reported a twenty-year individual therapy for a host of ailments—depression, anxiety, medical problems (including prostate cancer), and PTSD stemming from childhood. He anxiously mentioned the first marriage to a woman who was never emotionally invested in him and the traumatic loss of his only child in infancy. In asking what they wanted help with, each gave an entirely personal response. Mary listed many of Bob's faults—self-centered, financially secretive, stingy with their daughter, prone to temper tantrums, reclusive, and generally uncaring. Bob immediately focused on paying for their daughter's four-year college tuition, an indication he had changed. As Mary off-loaded her list of grievances, Bob would stay in the here-and-now. A typical exchange went like this:

Bob: This week we went to the theater and had a nice dinner. (pause)

Mary: That's what he does, he mentions one thing and completely ignores everything else; always the minutia. He leaves out the temper tantrum in Europe because he had to buy wine and made us miss our tour bus. Never takes responsibility.

Bob: It's not the way the way I remember it.

Mary: You had the tantrum and blamed me because I said we would be late, and you insisted you had all the time in the world. Did we miss the bus?

Bob: (Looking sheepish) Yes we missed the bus. I thought we had more time.

In this and other exchanges, not atypical for early sessions, the couple is in a quid pro quo debate over whose reality is the preferred version. This exchange is for the therapist as well; he is viewed by one or the other partner in a fixed role as an arbitrator, the one who decides who is right or wrong. Much in the way the couple is split between contemptuous feelings and the need to be right, the therapist is faced with what to do and how to think about their surface rendition. There is no marital and sparse individual history available as yet. We are given the conflictual opening exchange as it occurs in the "getting to know your situation" portion of assessment.

This question arises: what does the couple want from the therapist/therapy? We can pose several questions: "What do you suppose this exchange represents for the marriage over time?" "Clearly there are powerful differences in how each of you views the same situation. Both are quite frustrated with how needs are addressed in the marriage, being that you each see the same situation differently." The last question implies there is a depth of conflictual thinking beneath the couple surface expressions that has led the couple down a slippery slope threatening their continuing the marriage. Neither partner satisfies the other. There is deep anger in Mary, as she can go along with Bob only if she changes her sense of what is real. Bob tantrums because he cannot handle criticism when he becomes preoccupied with personal gratification. I silently wonder about his need for alcohol. The insistence on purchasing wine has consequences for missing their bus. Time for this couple harbors disaster, with Bob's cool indifference, perceptual distortion about needs, and a preoccupation for autonomy without the requisite capacity for sharing.

I have often pondered why some couples never move beyond surface presentations with their therapists? The obvious redundancies of complaints, sometimes contemptuously hurled, is usual for couples in trouble. Beginnings provide the couple with a space to freely talk, at times, in an evacuative mode, as a first step in searching out the therapist's role. In the previous example, the therapist functioned as listener to each partner's anger-driven and frustrated complaints. At first, it appeared nothing was required of the therapist beyond taking in Mary's angry complaints and Bob's more complex defenses, in which he partially acknowledged he was mistaken, but minimized the effects on the marriage.

If the couple continued to disagree for several sessions, and differences prevailed, some therapists, either by design or out of frustration, would break in and direct the couple to think of something nice to say. In an object relations framework, the couple is viewed as needing distance from other feelings, possibly more vulnerable ones, so the defensive nature of offensive expressions might be considered first before making an attempt to shift the couple away from their anger, until the therapist came up with a thought about the defensive function of the anger. We pair defense and anxiety as they lie beneath the angry exchanges, even though the angry disappointments are real enough to the couple. Anxiety about an ending therefore might be the issue, especially if one partner (Mary) is close to leaving the marriage. Thinking about deeper anxieties, the therapist might mention the large number of grievances on Mary's mind and ask the couple if there is any hope that some work might be accomplished, being that they had sought out the therapist. Depending on timing and motivation, the therapist might observe that Bob appeared to be a deer in headlights when Mary leveled her complaints. Clinical curiosity is about each partner's representation or style when communicating or receiving the other's negative feelings about the marriage and when being accused of failing. I asked the couple about seeking help and asked if there was any hope that we could have some time to understand what had happened to them. Bob had not yet expressed any complaints about Mary, instead taking the hits and insisting he loved her and wanted to make the marriage work.

I supposed the marital struggle presented to me might have to do with she wants out, he wants status quo, and she has to escalate her mission so he will relent and she can leave. However, I also wanted us to consider if Mary wished to be hopeful as a last ditch effort but it meant convincing Bob into changing his ways. A failed second marriage weighed heavily in the air. I was not feeling hopeful. There was much anger and bitterness in Mary, and seeming naïveté (related to passive-hostile dependency) coming from Bob.

The next chapter presents the object relations model in application to assessment and treatment of a polarized marriage. We bring the reader into the couple's "psychic space" and crippled marital container through transcribed conversations. We discover core couple unconscious dynamics that keep them stuck. We report how the therapist dealt with being negated and how countertransference analysis opened a potential space for healing.

Chapter Three

Object Relations Couple Therapy

Psychoanalytic couple therapy begins with a deceptively simple question: What do we make of each other? I will describe the object relations method and reproduce my clinical experiences as faithfully as possible. The caveat to the reader is that we can never know with certainty how the process of change occurs. For colleagues favoring hard evidence-based methods, object relations practice is not for the faint of heart. Writing about clinical practice is difficult because the process is always in flux. Writing from memory and notes serves as a best effort. I recognize my report is selective. It is easier to theorize practice than to demonstrate it. This is in part due to the clinical material that object relations therapists study and treat. We rely on imagining, or dreaming up, the clinical situation in terms of our individual valence for responding to unconscious processes. A colleague, Charles McCormack (2000), said treatment begins in the mind of the therapist.

I believe the couple is not a treatment couple from the start; their wounded lives make our treatment frame an ordeal. At the beginning of therapy, a couple presses for obfuscation, in order to prevent break down in their defensive system. We hold their terror of the frame in mind and provide a vantage point we hope they can take in. The therapist attempts to open the space for a new experience in which the future is not born of the past. Even though being listened to can initially produce relief, realizing that there is someone who might understand, the exposure to a stranger can be felt as dangerous or humiliating. The moment we think about the clinical experience *in situ,* it gets lost and replaced by another, perhaps more captivating, one that occurs later on. Due to the flow of a session, memories of what happened are incoherent at first. Comprehending what is going on in the room is affected by overloaded effects during couple exchanges. Highly emotional exchanges cause interruptions in our thinking and observing, and they challenge objectivity in deciding what is relevant to treatment. Subjective responses are common and we must surrender to their discomforts until we regain an analytic focus.

Philosophical arguments abound in psychoanalytic circles about the relevance of seeking objective truth about the human encounter. We can assume that the couple's experiential world is knowable via the structure of the treatment setting. Three minds are interacting within a frame; the frame functions as a laboratory of sorts, which is structured to permit our study of emotional pain and then provide a means for healing through an informed human response. My version of what happens in a couple's case may be flawed with countertransference stemming from the intimacy with the couple that I internalized, so I expect that my treatment and its results may be lacking hard "scientific" evidence. Object relations treatment features a use of self in which vague impressions, intuitive reactions, dream-like states, and empathic curiosity provide links to unconscious material (Bollas, 1987). To return to the framing question, this chapter is an in-depth consideration of what partners make of each other and us as we move from surface to depth.

THEORETICAL BASIS FOR IN-DEPTH TREATMENT

Object relations therapy places the unconscious field (Baranger and Baranger, 2008) or matrix of pathological relating at the center of our clinical attention. Object relations theory originated in Freud's fundamental discoveries of unconscious mental process and his elaborations of psychic structure. The Freudian approach to healing mental anguish focused on interpreting the individual patient's transference to the therapist from a position of nonjudgmental, objective interest. Treatment of unconsciously derived symptoms and disturbed character structures inevitably led clinicians after Freud to broaden their inquiry from the individual unconscious to the relationship between psychic determinism and environmental influences. Object relations couple therapy (ORCT) expands knowledge of individual unconscious object relations to the couple and family environments, based on the assumption that objects (intrapsychic versions of significant others) are internalized for life. The object relations approach to couples broadens clinical work without sacrificing depth in comprehending human relating and in couple conflict in particular.

Psychoanalytic theory was reworked by Fairbairn (1952), Guntrip (1961), Winnicott (1956), Bion (1962), and Klein (1948), among others. Expansion of object relations theory of the individual to the couple emerged from the original research of Henry Dicks in London (1967) and Bannister and Pincus (1964). Scharff and Scharff (1991) wrote the first complete theory and practice of ORCT, and Scharff and Bagnini (2001) later amplified the theory and range of practice applications of ORCT. ORCT has come of age and was third in the order of contemporary couple treatment methods listed in *The Clinical Handbook of Couple Therapy* 3rd edition, (Gurman and Jacobson, 2001). Various faculty of the Tavistock Centre for Couple Relations in Great Britain have expanded Kleinian and Bionian theory of the individual to the parental and marital couple and family. Many other clinicians in France, Australia, Italy, South Africa, Scotland, and elsewhere have contributed to a worldwide growing interest in expanding psychoanalytic thinking to treatment of couples.

In their seminal review of object relations theory, Greenberg and Mitchell (1983) reviewed Fairbairn's psychoanalytic perspective on personality development in his *Object Relations Theory of the Personality* (1954) and his reworking of Freudian drive theory. Fairbairn altered Freud's intrapsychic model of the mind by postulating that humans are motivated from the outset by more than instinctual drives. He proposes an intrapsychic-interpsychic psychoanalytic framework that contextualizes individual development as a two-person experience with the observation that humans are relationship-seeking from birth. Contemporary infant observation and attachment studies significantly amplify Bowlby's early work on infant attachment (1969, 1973), and Daniel Stern's (2005) work empirically demonstrates Fairbairn's earlier object relations view that human connecting occurs much earlier than previously thought and gratification of biological needs is only one component of human striving. Containing and metabolizing infant and child anxieties through parent reverie offers much more than the required safety and secure holding for well-being. When there is reasonable attunement to a child, frustration tolerance and affect regulation overlap, leading to integration of autonomous needs and recognition of others as having capabilities and limitations of their own. Individual development from this vantage point is a generative intrapsychic and relational process, with implications for marriage satisfaction, because an intimate bond requires two relatively autonomous individuals. In clinical assessments of couples presenting for help, we determine the extent to which a creative couple is available to bear the developmental push from childhood to adult intimacy requirements.

The opening question (What do we make of each other?) inevitably leads to the intrapsychic and interpsychic domains of human relating. Clinically we attend to those couple issues of lost, broken, and "ought" connections that impede human relatedness. Object relations practice theory conceptualizes couples as a unit expressing individual and conjoint conscious and unconscious relationship patterns that seek to recover or repair primary connections through marriage, but the couple becomes bogged down in phantasy-driven relating (we use the Kleinian use of "ph" instead of an "f," which would connote infantile motives such as symbiotic or hate-driven ties). When childhood motives for wholesome connecting were thwarted by disturbed family relations, the future became frozen by the overdetermined past. As a result of trauma and neglect, some couple's relational beliefs are centered in primitive and hurtful affects. Our treatment approach focuses on thwarted needs for connection, stemming from basic distrust and a lack of safety between the partners. We invite the couple to examine possible causes for current failures. Though a couple expects the therapist to fix one partner or the other, we offer another perspective that opens the space for thinking about the lost objects in the past (psychic history) and the potential for reworking losses through insight and reclaiming the self (Scharff, 1992).

The therapist's stance in an object relations approach consists of freely allowing the couple to share whatever they wish, following the affect or noting absent affect as each presents the particulars of what brought them into therapy. Rather than a structured interview, use of a genogram, or other paper and pencil tools, the object relations approach favors open communication untainted by therapist needs to directly structure conversation or prematurely prescribe a fix. First we want to understand the couple's unconscious and conscious fit. Unconscious communications of anxieties about being in therapy and prior object relations are the clinical material for deciding what to offer so the therapist is geared to a less-is-more approach—the therapist is a container and holder of the couple's need to express unpleasant and disturbing experiences. We try to provide a safe transitional space (Winnicott, 1971) in order to eventuate a potential space for new thinking and feeling, emerging from the couple's experience of the therapist as a good-enough object.

Couple treatment can heal old pain. We view disturbed marital behavior as a result of deep developmental calamities and deficits. Couple therapists in supervision often report their distress when affective discharge predominates early sessions and we quickly realize that the partner's individual and shared holding environment was compromised. When the partner's evacuative motives appear to predominate a couple's interactions, as in threatening to leave the marriage, blaming, shaming, or rejecting, we can assume an overdetermined inability to sublimate and accurately perceive the world outside the self. For example, a discharge of aggression followed by a partner's withdrawal alerts the therapist to take up the possibility of an unconscious couple-fit that generates the specific exchanges. The pressure on the therapist is great. "Don't just sit there; do something" is a standard feeling. Our approach is "Don't just do something precipitously, sit there," but realize that this is the couple's situation, and it may be *normal* for them, and we can ask if it is normal for them. We sit *and* actively listen for underlying anxiety or pain, determining a proper intervention or holding position, while containing their and our affects. In matters of physical or psychological safety, we of course act directly to diffuse an attack, sometimes by asking the less agitated partner to leave for a few minutes while we attempt to reach the attacking partner. Ours is not a passive approach. We note when spouses are highly aggressive, they may be unable to sustain marital therapy, as the exposure may be overwhelming. In such situations, we can stop the process and recommend individual therapy, medication, or anger management, among other choices. Later on, we might resume the couple treatment.

To accomplish the above we study transferences and counter-transference in the work. Our clinical emphasis on discovering unknown developmental disturbances and naming prior relationship breakdowns presses the therapist into the center of the couple's feared and foreboding previous objects. By taking on the inner world of the couple, we have to bear the couple's object sorting by becoming transference figures. Is the therapist unconsciously perceived as an older brother who abandoned one of the partners, a lost lover, or a vengeful part of the spouse's self that is waiting to be unleashed onto the well-meaning therapist? Bad object relations repeat themselves in therapy sessions (through sudden transference reactions to the therapist's holding) in the normal process of opening space for new experience. We will suffer when merely asking the couple to question long-held beliefs. Impulsive reactions are likely to occur when questioning the parameters and derivatives of fixed knowledge. Fixed knowledge refers to rigidly derived beliefs about reality. We provide a new object experience by containment of anxieties; however, inherent in an exploration of fixed ways of thinking, the therapist cannot always maintain an open space for thinking about and processing the resulting emotional reactions. An adage in couple work is, "If you want to understand an individual's personality, look for the company they keep."

What we make of each other pertains to the interplay of partners over time as each presses the other to conform to unconscious phantasies while (paradoxically) attempting to meet adult marital needs. What we make of each other involves a two-person psychological treatment in which we track projective identifications (Klein, 1952; Ogden, 1982) emerging from the partners' powerful affectively charged communications that seek accommodation and a congruent response from the other. Projections range from relatively benign to psychotic in regressed couples with undifferentiated relatedness. We adapt Klein's (1948) designation of the pathological problem as insufficient integration of paranoid-schizoid and depressive positions. Couples present baffling levels of disorganized thinking and emotional distortion and require from the therapist (in order to work through their problems) depressive-position capabilities and a higher level of processing self- and other-distortions. Couples stuck in a paranoid-schizoid position co-project in alarming and wild formats. They need a language that detoxifies persecutory feelings and addresses retaliation in the form of withdrawal or rage, and an attitude of openness to understanding to counter avoidance and denial, which defend against self fragmentation.

We also study marital issues with regard to intergenerational transmissions of pathology. In this way, we can locate and reframe the links between intrapsychic developmental lines of catastrophe (individual histories) and interpsychic (couple mental states) when repeated in the marriage, by noticing how they are re-enacted with us in the transference. We believe the interpsychic aspects (the spouses' unconscious communications as a couple) involve two minds, as each partner carries an intrapsychic load of an affectively charged phantasy, including extremes of aggressive and libidinal/loving aims. Within the interpsychic space of the two minds is overburdened by deep unconscious conflicts, unmet longings and unrecognized and unmourned losses are held in dynamic tension and are sensitive to triggering moments by one's partner, which lead to emotional spillovers as projections replay each partner's earlier relational patterns. We use a language of relevance between the here-and-now repetitions to tap into each partner's unconscious history. A here-and-now interpretive emphasis implies there had to be a there and then pattern that is continuing to wreak havoc (Grotstein, 2007).

We speak from a position of empathic curiosity and imagine possibilities about couple fit, rather than speaking as though we have the answers as undeniable facts. We empathize with what has put the partners at risk by referring to the repetitions of earlier deficient or traumatizing patterns centered in parent-child relating repeated in the present. These patterns may include abuse, neglect, and brainwashing in the sense that the child's view of reality was negated or reframed entirely according to parent-driven malignant projections of the paranoid/persecutory type. We are especially interested in determining maladaptive dissociative patterns that re-surfaced in conflict over one's choice of a mate soon after the marriage ceremony, or after the birth of a first child. Old destruc-tive patterns can surface if the marriage was attempted as a cure for life's challenges or if there was a set of conscious or unconscious infantile fantasies that inevitably prevented a reasonable adult give and take, due to especially low or high levels of emotional dis-charge or fluctuation. The above patterns of rigidity or fluctuation have been addressed in the clinical literature on pathogenic couple fits encountered in treatment: borderline (Lachkar, 1992, McCor-mack, 2000; Slipp, 1984), obsessional (Barnett, 1975), masochistic (Glickhauf-Hughes and Wells, 1995) or narcissistic fits (Scharff and Bagnini, 2004; Solomon, 1989).

We recognize and are open to receiving patient unconscious communication, striving to organize our emotional responses and mentalizing primitive intrapsychic process. Receptivity begins in the therapist's mind, including interpreting dream material (Bagni-ni, 2000, 2006) and by encouraging associations, and when encoun-tering transferences. We are comfortable working from present to past and vice versa to elaborate psychological defenses, hidden anxieties, and ego structures. We take note of lifespan-specific de-velopmental failures, unprocessed losses, and unmetabolized emo-tions. Lifespan passages receive a great deal of attention, as these experiences influence and predetermine marital and self expecta-tions; for example, the way one navigates phases of life can gener-ate continued unconscious expectations for a return of traumatic exposure, generating unconscious fantasies of magical repair from one's partner. Clinical attention is paid to several transferences in

the treatment field—between partners and between each partner
and the therapist. Another transference dimension is the couple as a
unit of two who relate to the therapist as a complex object for use.

A countertransference error occurs when processing regressed
couple transferences. We may become confused when concrete ideas abound about who is at fault for marital distress. For example, a
"you versus me" repetition requires sensitive handling with firm
confrontation. Each partner may be testing the therapist as a side-
taker, because that would reduce the couple's polarized state of
mind. For partner A, if the therapist takes my side, for instance, that
may temporarily reduce the futility of always feeling wrong or at
fault. However, that position puts all the blame on the other partner
who is excluded from the preferred dyad; couples leave therapy at
this point if the therapist is not monitoring the countertransference,
and takes sides; one partner becomes the therapist's favorite, which
results in a failure in the couple format that becomes rationalized
into an individual therapy case. We might conjecture an oedipal
victory (Britton, 1990) for one partner and an oedipal loss for the
other, which repeats the winner or loser dynamic in the families of
origin; countertransference has to be monitored to prevent a couple
impasse. Couples in regression may have not developmentally
achieved a normative oedipal position, in that they cannot tolerate
any third in the other partner's life—a child, a friendship, a career,
the therapist, or differences per se. These impasses are experienced
as narcissistic wounds in the form of rejection, abandonment, or
worse, destructive to a continuity of self-esteem. For partners with
pre-oedipal object relations pathology, the primary dyad is the site
of greatest deficit, trauma or neglect; consequently marriage is expected to make up for the losses without any recognition of the
contributions of past life to current unrealistic demands. Another
important component of the work involves the therapist's personality and sensitivity. Psychoanalytic approaches focus on unconscious resonance between the world of the couple and the experi-

ence of the therapist. The object relations couple techniques (which include here-and-now and reconstructive interpretations, uncovering of multiple motives, and revisiting and mourning losses) intersect at the boundary between the couple's unconscious awareness and the couple therapist's reflections in a triangular field. Each participant in the treatment triangle is exposed to emotional and mental repercussions during highly charged sessions.

Turmoil often results from unmetabolized childhood disturbances. Regressed couples often fear breakdown and abandonment. We encounter couples with a range of fission and fusion terrors—in fusion situations, a partner carries a deep lack of reliable self structure so that another is sought who appears more individuated and with whom closeness might complete the fragile parts of the self needed for well-being. Fear of fusion occurs when partners fear losing their individuality. These partners are threatened by others' needs.

The clinical emphasis is twofold: We track individual personalities while keeping in mind the ways anxieties and defenses are dealt with by the couple as a unit. Repetitive behaviors can reveal unconscious parallels that are unknown to the couple; for example, abandonment anxieties in each partner can result in acquiescence or clinging. Each partner has developmental strengths and weaknesses that impinge on marital development and intimate connecting. For an object relations therapist, the couple's overt interactions are less central to the field of study and treatment. Until the couple is helped to recognize and deal with the unconscious aspects of human experience that followed them into the current relationship, they may go on functioning as best they can, but marital and self-satisfaction will be compromised, as partners repeat emotionally overwhelming difficulties of deficient nurturing and as trauma replays itself concretely and is automatically ascribed to the other partner's indifference or demanding ways. We enlarge the dyadic field to the triadic to include the therapist. We add group ideas

(Bion, 1961) that expand attunement to multiple transferences and their complementarity—the unconscious fit between the partners' individual personalities and the *couple state of mind*, which is transmitted in the therapy space on a session-by-session basis. The couple state of mind is a concept of two intermingled personalities. We use this conceptual tool in which we listen carefully to the ways the couple communicates unconscious process through content. Individual attitudes and approaches to marital problems are observed from the standpoint of the extent to which the pair is "we" oriented. Is the couple speaking in unison, as in "one voice," or polarized, with different versions of events or situations of concern? One typical couple style commonly encountered is enmeshment that is caused by fear of abandonment; autonomy is sacrificed in favor of compliance. This couple type coheres to defeat the therapist's attempts to determine the couple's capacity for individual difference; this capacity can help couples manage and identify conflict. If a couple appears to have little tolerance for conflict, we wonder why they seek therapy. Couples with the aforementioned pattern might present about an acting out teenager, individual symptoms (e.g., depression), or employment difficulties. A different couple pattern is an overly individuated partnership, which involves fear of coming together in a merger of selves; this pattern is the reverse of the previous style. These couples approach the therapist with differences so great that one wonders how they have any common ground for intimate relating.

A hybrid of the two is sometimes encountered in the form of a fluctuating couple that may (in the course of a single session or over many sessions) oscillate between pseudo-cooperation and icy distancing. I call these couples "icy hot," to describe the oscillation between guarded involvement and polarization. These couples fluctuate between the paranoid-schizoid and depressive positions (Klein, 1952), in which pseudo-cooperative efforts occur but the couple returns to prior modes of relating when unpleasant topics come into view (e.g., when a partner's defenses against closeness is questioned or when a confrontation occurs over refusal to allow for different viewpoints). Unlike the middle phase of couple treatment, when movement into awareness can be tolerated and projective stances are not as rigid or automatic, these couples' hard-wired positions are repeated many times, and the therapist's attempts to interfere too quickly (usually out of frustration) will go nowhere.

The couple may then turn on the therapist, who has lost the ability to monitor, and empathize with the couple's retreat when anxieties are used defensively. At these times, the therapist is perceived as a deficient object, or as too demanding, temporarily reducing the couple's interpersonal feud. The triangle is thought about transferentially as is the dyad in psychoanalysis, because both fields are considered a rich source of meaning. Triangular transferences are more problematic because more data is oscillating and difficult to track, as in group therapy. However, the available (Scharff and Scharff, 1991) theory assists the therapist in discovering where he is located in the projective maze or gridlock (Morgan, 1995), retaining a level of freedom to recover from the seductions and isolations that emanate from couple's utilization of his or her personality.

Past lives have preempted the couple's ability to emotionally and safely bond or grow. Problem solving is less a feature of unconscious couple work, and we work on personality change to a sufficient extent to rework the more destructive projected parts of each partner in a benign way. Bad experiences must be survived by the therapist with severely disordered couples for whom trust is an impediment to couple therapy and marital improvement.

An honest therapist will acknowledge a preference for an idealized transference, however short-lived. The therapist can easily become a bad object too (e.g., distrusted). A partner may become overwhelmed by the prospect of never being empathized with, or if empathy occurs between the other partner and the therapist it may trigger sadomasochistic or murderous sibling rivalry or oedipal rejection. If inherent fears of becoming disarmed by empathy are not addressed, the therapist can be persecuted for his or her thinking when a partner insists the therapist take sides or when the therapist is representing the couple relationship. A partner may demand side-taking due to intolerance of the threesome.

Regressed couples differ from more flexible ones when there is a departure from therapist dyadic relating—partner-therapist communication. The difference between focusing on the individual and focusing on the couple is no simple matter. If the therapist prematurely observes the couple as a unit so as to indicate a shared perspective or belief, one partner may feel threatened with merger anxieties and behave as though there is no differentiation; the defense is driven by a fear of engulfment. The assessment process will, of necessity, require adjustments due to aspects of disturbance in relating. We can infer from this example that historically significant impediments prevent one or both partners from imagining common relationship anxieties and sharing them with the therapist.

The case study illustrates assessment and treatment pitfalls in holding and containment. Progress emerged as a result of unexpected encounters and discoveries that are inherent to the object relations open systems approach.

CASE STUDY

The Couple: Assessment Phase and Early Impressions

Janis (J.), age 42, and Greg (G.), age 41. Caucasian; married 10 years; son, age 8; daughter, age 9.

Employment

G. is an underemployed business consultant. They sought therapy due to angry exchanges over differences in needs and the break-down in goodwill between them.

J. is an overemployed and burdened pediatric nurse and midwife. The couple moved to their current locale five years ago to be closer to J.'s family. They mutually chose to purchase a large home in need of extensive renovations, but finances slowed the construction process to the extent that the couple fights over the slow pace. G. is at home and is the house-parent who does the repairs and sub-contracting. They sought help due to angry exchanges and power struggles about discrepancies in individual needs and expectations:

J.: House not getting finished—renovated rooms for each child, a family room, and exterior painting.

G.: House-husband, doing what he can but can't stand the nagging. When in conflict, he blows up and withdraws while she pursues and vents how hurt she is. The sword and the net: He pulls the sword (anger) out and takes a quick swipe, and she throws the net by pursuing him with the evacuation of hurts.

Family Background

G.: International corporate banking family with high-ranking CEO father and grandfather; G. is only one who chose another career that was not supported but tolerated. Mother anxious and invested in outside volunteer work during husband's long absences traveling on business.

J.: Professionals—law, teaching, engineering. She was expected to become a pharmacist, but chose pediatric nursing after quitting pharmacy school. J.'s younger brother, S., has mental, social, and emotional disabilities. Her family supports him. S. has a history of poor choices of women, an unemployment record, and a leech-like reliance on family, which creates ongoing parental worry about what happens after their parents die. S. creates controversy with the couple. J. appears empathically enmeshed, G. with a more tough-love attitude, as in "shape up and less coddling." Moral tirade from G.; J. feels isolated and feels like no one gets it (viz., how sad she is for her brother), and G. is unsympathetic.

G. fears they will have the responsibility of taking care of S. after the parents die.

S. is living in the mountains of Utah with a much older woman with an eighteen-year-old son, whom they suspect abuses hard drugs; this son frightened their daughter on a family visit. The couple feels betrayed, having made their best efforts, but J. cannot bring herself to share the outrage about brother with her family.

Object Relations Initial Couple Assessment

Projective Matrix

Complementary projective identifications in which disowned contributions to the conflicts are ascribed to the other's inadequacies. Narcissistic wounds justify blame and self-interest (J. Scharff and Bagnini, 2004), minimizing awareness of each partner's participation and co-construction of marital interchanges as basic to breakdown.

Early Hypothesis

Unexplored object relations complementarity in which the couple feels concretely exploited and victimized by the other, but unconsciously holds traumatic encapsulation, imploded helplessness, and the experience of being sucked dry by the other, which they react to through G.'s explosive anger (when he is nagged) and J.'s imploded depressive state of constant hurt. S. is an emotional catalyst for the couple impasse, but family-of-origin material will cast more light on the intensity of their impasse. I suspect they are in a joint paranoid-schizoid state, regressive and needing careful listening, with minimal interpretation, which would be experienced as saturating and intrusive. The dyadic patterns of interacting with me and the impasse establishes the hypothesis and working position of attunement and use of titrated comments to each. For now, I attend to their versions of the couple problems, providing a space for curiosity for more elaboration and detail. I apply a calm listening stance and point out when there is an overload of hurt that the other partner reacts to with anger. I am slowing down the more powerful reactions, not by directly intervening or preventing but by commenting on the level of helplessness the fighting causes. I also imply there is more to their story and I am interested in any background information that could predate the current distress. They do not respond to my comments directly but go on with the fighting and struggling. Slowly I notice they are looking to me at moments when they sense the futility of the fighting. I nod in recognition of this new accomplishment. Object relations couple technique recognizes that containment is primary in providing a safe opportunity for exploration of salient issues underpinning current conflicts. Accepting each partner is suffering from polarized affect but cannot find a way through it, due to anger over hurts and disappointments, requires listening that accepts the polarized versions as their shared reality. The therapist, however, holds onto the view that a potentially therapeutic version may be found if the containment is successful.

Background to Session 8

Clinical Aim in Early Phase: Detoxifying Core Relational Impasse

Due to attentive holding, the three previous weeks were calmer, and they were able to discuss differences without resorting to attack and defense. They were still self-focused, and not comfortable as a couple, seeking attunement from me in a dyadic preference—each communicated directly to me, though occasionally I would address something to them as a pair, such as, "You are both carrying the disappointments of expecting a better return for the move closer to J.'s parents." Neither responded to the statement, implying that they could not consider what they mutually carried; however, J. reported that G. was not bailing out when she came home with questions about his day, about the children, but mostly about progress on the house. G. reported that J. wasn't all over him lately with her fault finding when he explained his efforts. I had redirected the self-defensive and offensive exchanges through mirroring unrealistic hopes and shared disappointments along the time line of leaving their previous home for this new adventure and having their second child during the transition. The deeper rift around failed dependency needs was closer to the surface, and it predated the current complaints. We were beginning to explore their perspectives that might explain the weakening of their bond (container) before they move closer to her parents and farther away from G.'s. They did not expect to have a second child so soon after the move. I had them reprocess a disappointment. J.'s family did not embrace the second pregnancy, being slightly critical they had so much work to do on the house. The couple had to rely on each other through the pregnancy and after the birth. J.'s parents eventually connected with the second grandchild, but the couple was stressed by the critical stance of J.'s parents about the timing of the first.

Clinical note: The couple was unable to respond to my empathically reframing that they share disappointments that may not be one partner's fault but rather occur as a result of a joint decision—my motive was to detoxify the conflicts in favor of examining phantasies about failed expectations with the hope of partially reducing the impasse fueled by projections: J. blames G., and he counter blames J. for relentless demands. The therapeutic aim is not that the couple will take in the statement wholesale and appreciate the therapist's "wisdom" but rather that the couple will unconsciously internalize the comment for later use when they can empathize with each other. If the therapist's holding is trusted, the internalization can occur.

Session 8: A Transference Disaster and Recovery

J. shifted from the usual reporting about the week's events—her saturation from many child pediatric cases, not enough time with the children, and ongoing financial burdens—to the topic of her younger brother, S.

S. had fallen into yet another dangerous relationship with a woman, who was making him spend all his money to refurbish her house (a parallel to the treatment couple situation). J.'s intensity was pressing hard on me, as her tears and words increased from the moment she began, the words flowing without let up. G. was listening quietly, watching J. and me, and I noticed his hands curl into tension-filled fists, I thought, in combat mode. I imagined that he feels this way when he can't protect J., or himself from her acting out and her impervious brother; I felt myself in a parallel state, identifying with the couple. A while later I surmised G. was also identified with the brother-in-law's chronic unemployment and G. feared that J.'s retaliation would be displaced on G. soon enough.

In my mind, the longstanding significance of J.'s brother to the couple was represented by an exploitive use of the object while appearing helpless. While sucking out the resources of a good-hearted but guilt-ridden family, S. had not learned self-reliance. I silently thought the waste of good resources appeared to be stored in the couple's unconsciously shared identification with S., and that they were the sacrificial object for each other. G. knew about exploitation from his childhood I suspected, but J. appeared so distraught and helpless that she was not in touch with much else.

J. was preoccupied. I silently wondered how this new material on her brother could shed light on G.'s recent failures to support her (emotionally and financially). Feeling somewhat split, I (like J.) was not angry at her brother's drain on the family resources and emotions. G. had until recently borne the brunt of her deep hurts. G. had been receiving the brunt of the "tough love" from J. that she could not apply to her parents or siblings. G. was not equipped to express his fears of underachieving, which I supposed were due to carrying earlier guilt about having disappointed his family of origin by declining a high-level banking career.

J. paused to reach for tissues. Here was a moment to speak to the couple. I offered the thought that her family situation seemed quite desperate and long-term—could this be adding to the continued fallout about G.'s unemployment?

G. chimed in for the first time in the session about his having been invited to participate in family talks in which no one seemed angry about S.'s selfish ways. They expressed upset and worry, but kept giving in to him. G. was getting angry at this point, pressing forward that he would just cut him off if he did not account for his behavior. J., who was drying her tears, then turned on me with, "Are you listening to him?" "My family feels very badly about brother but my parents cannot cut him off." More tears were mixing with anger. "I bet you think we should cut him off and let him starve." J. had assumed that G. and I were aligned against her family. In J.'s paralysis, fears had been internalized for years, and differentiation was impossible. I asked her to say more about her experience of me.

She was in an angry confrontation with me. She was questioning my neutrality, which she felt was undermined by a personal agenda against her brother. I felt I was losing ground/credibility rapidly and might lose J.'s trust. At the same time, my role as a perceived neutral mediator was in need of revision too, because J.'s unconscious anxieties needed to be expressed. We were enacting the polarized couple relationship—a stalemate, with a loss of trust and safety. The new affect represented victimization, the passive-aggressive form of narcissistic motives in her brother's longstanding behavior. She could not as yet process the salient lifelong effects. I was in the eye of a storm of unexamined beliefs. Being that G. was listening attentively, I felt J. might fear we were in collusion. I thought that G. was expecting J.'s wrath to return to him soon enough, and he was appreciating my taking it on for him. I thought it was safer for J. too, as I was not retaliating.

We were enacting a *me-versus-you* split. Such a part-object has one aim—self-preservation, "you are with me or against me." Here was the *fusion of oneness* within the martyr's impasse, and I was the one tested. I wanted to take her on, I thought. After all, wasn't I entitled to a fair evaluation of my mostly benign motives?
The following are defensive characteristics of narcissistic individuals with rigid beliefs:

1. The illusion of sanity in the absence of doubt. If doubt exists, there is a loss of omnipotence or its veneer.
2. A nonreceiver of truth as an object relationship (a blank wall).

I felt the slavish dependency that J. was projecting—either I am with or against her, much in the way G. was experiencing J.'s fixed view of her and her brother's entitlement to receive boundless support. There was no room to explore a new idea: that feeling trapped in a pity pot, and resorting to a bitter bank (pity as an entitlement and bitterness as retaliation) had no currency because of J.'s repressed guilt-ridden superego. G.'s approach was too brutal for J. She couldn't take it in from him.

I decided to reframe G.'s approach and take on her view of me simultaneously. I said,

> J., I am taking on your anger, but the helplessness behind it is
> felt by your husband and you. G. does become angry, and you
> are afraid to be angry about your brother's ways. You mutually
> feel used and helpless even though there is no solution as yet
> about your brother, but your fears of giving up on him go deep.
> You and G. react to the situation quite personally, each believ-
> ing the situation from only one point of view. You aren't able to
> safely share each other's view because each of you is threatened
> about what his behavior brings out in your partner. Your brother
> takes a toll on your marriage as long as you refuse to see the
> common helplessness you both share beneath your stalemate.

J. broke down tearfully and shared she has always felt badly about
succeeding while her brother floundered. She could not access anger, but we had temporarily diffused our impasse and had new
material for discussion. G. became softer, having just heard for the
first time that J. had felt like an overachiever and was never comfortable with it because her parents were so caught up with helping
her damaged brother.

Middle Phase—Working Couple

Session 17

Illustration of Therapist and Couple Tracking and Reframing Projective Identifications

The couple was in conversation about financial burdens, which had
previously polarized them. Each partner felt victimized by the other's stated sacrifices and burdened by who did the most because of
so little recognition or appreciation for their efforts. I had just
pointed out that they both made efforts that did not seem to bring
them together in recognition as a working partnership. I was curious about their emphasis on differences. What emerged was G.'s
sense that whatever he did would not be considered good enough
by J. His fears of failing her brought out his resentment that her

demands were unreasonable. She took up the question of whether she was demanding, a dim awareness, and explored the possibility that she was clinging to an old pattern in which her role in life was to assist others without expecting recognition; could she be repeating that with G., who was not taking to it as she had done in childhood. I thought she was speaking of a hidden projected part of herself. G. had reacted to J. with anger and resentment, emotions that she could not be in touch with in regard to her family of origin. He carried the resentment for her, but his fear of failing her had also become a new discovery that they both began to consider.

The couple had been unable to process these juxtaposed dynamic issues: fear of failure fused with resentment for unreasonable demands for sacrifice. I indicated that they might be suffering from a shared feeling that sacrifice in childhood must never be resented. They were so often deadlocked because they had no conception of a working couple who could benignly resent sacrifice. They had not realized their fears of failure and resentment of parents who they each served without much acknowledgment. They blamed each other for repressed losses associated with a lack of good-enough parent-child relationships. They acted out their resentments on each other. Unacknowledged loss kept them polarized (similar to their childhood experience). The new question in the room was why were they not recognizing and appreciating the other one as part of a working couple? We began to trace the malignant projective material to identifications with their parents as controlling, neglectful, and needy objects. Neither partner had internalized a parent who admired and appreciated them—a parallel process in each of their families of origin. Also, each partner was behaving as a wounded subject. They viewed their individual contributions as inadequate, which added to the doubts of a committed future, which had some validity, considering G.'s underemployment. We explored resentments toward parents that were hidden and consequently were projected into the marital relationship. G. and J. lacked the emotional

security needed in marriage. I reframed the language of unappre-
ciated work and sacrifice, which produced deadlock to a language
of shaky emotional security and longstanding unmet appreciation.
They took in the language I offered and then explored relevant
childhood situations that related to current couple strife, specifically the splintered love relations with parents they had not previously
thought about.

Later in the session, I had an opportunity to reframe a projective
gridlock. Each partner was lamenting (an accomplishment in itself,
being that they were sharing common disappointments with less
attacking and defending—the usual fixed positions) over the lack
of time for couple enrichment.

J.: I love horseback-riding lessons and dancing, but we can't
afford them and G. doesn't think he's good at dancing. [I noted
that she was not focused on horseback riding, a solitary activity,
but was attempting conversation about a joint activity.]

G.: I said [getting agitated] I would arrange for dance lessons,
but you never give me times you can be available [looking plain-
tively at me]. I told you I'm not comfortable dancing, but I will
do it if you want to. You see [looking at me and looking resent-
ful] that it's never good enough?

J.:[Tearing up] I have no time to plan it myself. [Here J. undermines his "effort" to appease. I am thinking she no more willing
than he is, so she cannot risk receiving his less-than-100 percent
effort. They will pay for it later, assuming he is sacrificing
again. His insecurity as a dancer (potent male) is not noted either, due to J.'s deprived feelings.]

Me: I see this exchange as a roadblock. There is a discussion
about enjoying something together, soon after we open up about
painful childhood sacrificing; I sense that we again are right in

the center of sacrifice over enjoyment. J. can't let you try arrang-
ing an activity in which she might have to lead. In dancing, you
can't both be in charge. You're not comfortable, G., but willing.
J. seems reluctant too, while hinting it could be fun. I don't think
you're both talking about affordability; it's more about affording
a risk at being close again. I have a fantasy about a couple in
their living room. The kids are asleep, they turn on the music,
and they dance. They're not comfortable; it has been so long, but
there they are, and it costs nothing, yet a lot—they have to lower
their guard, just a bit in order to relocate trust.

J. and G. look at each other and laugh with relief and slight embarrassment. They leave the session a bit lighter. G. helps J. on with
her coat. J. offers G. a Lifesaver from my candy dish. He accepts a
red one. I wonder if my fantasy is corrective too soon. Will I pay
for it next session?

I then think it was only my fantasy, not a requirement, that they
go home and do it. I am not sure, feeling a little guilty even with the
comforting thought "only my fantasy."

Interventions were determined by therapist mindfulness, of
which type of couple fit was determined to need a particular approach. To accomplish a couple assessment and proper treatment
decision, we favored two modes of psychological capability for the
therapist from which technique emerged—sufficient detachment to
take in the observable patterns (clinical objectivity) and the use of
emotional reverie (subjective resonance to affect and regression) in
the form of unconscious empathic understanding by identifying
with the couple's internal object relationships. We clinically
learned from experience (Bion, 1962) and attempted to promote
couple learning, which had parallel elements. *Experience* refers to
perceptions, affects, memories, associations, sharing dream states,
spontaneous gestures, and phantasies. Learning occurred from analyzing and empathically relating to repeated communications and
resulted from the exchanges between the couple and therapist's

minds and emerging emotions. The analytic third (Ogden, 1982; Grotstein, 2007) describes the gestalt of the three interacting minds searching for illumination of and release from projective identification. Successful therapy involved a gradual transformative process that emerged from the investment of all participants. We can never be sure how the transformative process happened.

BENEFITS OF THE OBJECT RELATIONS APPROACH

The case and sessions illustrated the ways a couple benefited from the reframing of a conflictual impasse to a reflective approach to marital and interpsychic problems. The middle phase of treatment was not so much a clear movement through a high-conflict-pathological boundary to better containment, reflecting, and the taking back of malignant projections. Internalizing a new experience is not a scientific entity. The couple is an emotional container, subject to fluctuations between regressive and integrative motives. However, the object relations frame facilitated a therapeutic process. We provided a powerful tool in which we created new space for meaning-making and cathexis of old object relationships. At first, the deeply unconsciously-held beliefs were repeated in the transference, with the couple as a unit projecting onto the therapist. We demonstrated countertransference analysis, which made unconscious use of the therapist's analytic sensibility available for conscious sorting and comparing object usage; the couple made use of the new experience to reduce projective identifications. Unconscious calamities were open to review. Therapist empathic curiosity enabled the couple to re-metabolize significant distorted beliefs for use. Over time the couple felt safer and less subject to humiliation for infantile needs. The therapist's accepting stance with each partner established their capacity for tolerating the hurt and aggression each could not previously moderate. Affects that were not safe to express, such as childhood pain, and adult disappointments with parents, emerged and freed the couple from the marital gridlock.

With less polarization and improved couple containment, the couple was eventually able to work with sexual issues over a one-year period. I usually ask about the physical relationship in couple therapy, but the couple was so raw with hurt, anger, and impasse that I had to wait until progress was made. J. had a significant fear of being physically touched, stemming from incest when she was a teen. J.'s unwillingness to allow G. to plan for dance lessons made sense in light of this information. For his part, G. had been unable to "dance" (sexual potency) due to castration fears associated with childhood exposure to mother's hysterical and punitive outbursts while his father was away. The couple learned about each other's inhibited sexual motives through sharing childhood precursors. The issues could be worked with only after sufficient trust was established with me. The therapy lasted two years and focused entirely on couple sessions. I believe we would not have been able to safely address the sexual issues had we not laid the groundwork in the prior phases.

What *did* we make of each other? I reshaped my original framing question at the close of this section (not surprisingly) into the past tense. Retrospectively, the regressed couple affected the way I worked, due to transference repetitions that at first closed opportunities for exploring. The work of tracking and listening opened space for speaking about the stalemate and the underlying fears in terms of common unprocessed losses and their related inhibited affects. The result of in-depth understanding brought out meaningful links regarding unconscious fit (*folie a deux*—madness of two individuals merging unconscious traumatic experience). We worked with their emotional reactions to each other and to me to establish fresh understanding of longstanding patterns that originated in childhood and that continued to cause marital impasse. I tracked my countertransference experience, using aspects of it as I became consciously able to process and communicate back without attacking the couple or ignoring their use of me. I have shared only a portion of the clinical experience to demonstrate the working in-depth treatment method.

Working effectively with this couple would not have been possible had I dealt only with behavior and allowed the couple transferences to go unnoticed. I chose to work directly with transference and, in particular, detoxified projective identifications and their origins in family relations. Winning trust was difficult, but the approach underscored the way that patient listening to affect presented a way into the pain the spouses had in common, but could not empathize with, given their angry defenses and narcissistic self-preoccupations. We reduced the victimization each felt by expanding the field of exploration and meaning-making, thereby altering their fixed views.

Chapter Four

Types of Marriages Encountered in Couple Treatment

It is important when working from surface to depth to find out about internalized couples (object relationships) that we are encountering because conscious longings and conflicts join with unconscious wounded child parts that can affect being in therapy. I commonly treat three types of marriages during an average week of practice. I describe the central characteristics of each type, some theoretical ideas that guided how I understood each case (ideas that differentiated these couples), and what clinical requirements determined the treatment. The three types are the *wished-for marriage,* the *defensive marriage,* and the *split-off marriage.* These are by no means conscious couple choices, nor are these types intended to encompass all the varieties of couple tendencies. And types sometimes overlap.

Types offer conceptual tools from which the therapist can assess where a couple lies on the spectrum of couple regression versus mature relatedness and then select an appropriate technique. In every couple situation, holding and containment are crucial, but we learn to modify our technique to match up our use of self, according to the specific behaviors, attitudes, beliefs, communication styles, defenses, and anxieties present. The couple types I will describe are the result of studying and being affected by many couple object relations sets over time out of which projective processes embodied particular aspects that stood out and guided the work. I suggest we consider the types reported in this chapter not so much as the result of a formal research, but as a product of selective clinical attention over many years of couple work that has made a difference in guiding technique for a positive outcome.

A CAVEAT

Couple types can be studied separately or quantified as a model. I encourage couple therapists to recognize patterns that stand out with a particular couple in order to individualize the treatment. A large group of couples have demonstrated common clinical features that guide clinical focus and inform technique. Focusing on particular anxieties, defenses, maladaptive strategies, and interpersonal styles allows a therapist to move from a less random attunement to personality or couple tendencies to specific features. I have remained open to discovering each couple as they emerged in particular conscious and unconscious ways and have noticed types of common couple coping patterns as they caught my attention. A model, therefore, should be taken up as an exercise in organizing dynamic material in a comprehensive way; use of a model is a training tool, not intended as a substitute for openness to what occurs in each particular experience with a couple. As stated, we will study different types of couples for their unique clinical features and treatment requirements, but the three types could also be studied for their commonalities as a tentative model for learning psychoanalytic object relations treatment. We use a psychoanalytic expansion from theory of the individual to the couple to inform technique across the range of couple types. We focus on unconscious intrapsychic (within the individual psyche) and interpsychic (from one mind to the other) and affects as significant dynamics that guide the work. Holding and containment are core technical resources in individual psychoanalysis and are indispensable for assessing and treating couples.

THE WISHED-FOR MARRIAGE

This couple type refers to a normal phase in courtship *or* to a prolonged, unrealistic, fantasy-driven orientation to love relations. Dominant themes of romance, psychosomatic partnership, and psychosexual intimacy produce considerable closeness and a sense of "we-ness." The *psychosomatic partnership*, originally developed by Winnicott (1971), refers to all levels of physical touch experienced by spouses in their family from birth on. Prior satisfying, frustrating, or traumatic touch experiences predetermine the capacities of the spouses to enjoy the pleasures of giving and receiving affection. Psychosexual intimacy is a genital extension of the psychosomatic partnership, which depends on how each spouse's previous touch experiences were internalized. Adolescent and adult development would test the capacity for erogenous and genital touching of oneself and one's spouse, including mutual pleasuring, intercourse, and orgasm. Unlike more mature marriages, touch in the wished-for marital relationship is front-loaded with heightened excitability. There is fantasy-driven intensity, and early romance is usually a veneer for narcissistic merger fantasies. The sexual excitement functions to seal off anxieties about individual differences and to allay abandonment fears. Autonomous strivings are often subordinated to merger fantasies and togetherness.

As the wished-for marriage progresses beyond courtship, the couple has difficulty meeting, or moderating, the fantasy elements in favor of serious, intelligent work in the face of external demands. One example of distress in a conflicted relationship occurs when the couple is separated and each spouse must function independently. Another occurs when a child comes into the family and sharing the "realities" of infant dependency requires sublimating individual needs for the sake of a larger goal of making space for parenting.

Infantile reliance on unconscious wishes or cravings leads to conflict in meeting real-world requirements. The couple over relies on sentimentality and identification with past pleasures. Pathogenic couple adjustments outweigh developmental needs and inhibit the couple's maturation. When unconscious spousal histories emerge, they reveal a heavy investment in wish fulfillment, which clouds adaptive requirements, such as accepting limitations and losses; in the couple's unconscious, the flow of time itself seems irrelevant or downright terrifying. Bliss cannot last. Togetherness dreams and fantasies propel but are poor skill providers. These couples enter therapy lost and disillusioned. They suffer powerful ambivalences reactivated by unresolved oedipal wishes; they may compete with children for nurturing supplies.

CASE ILLUSTRATION

Carol (26) and Jim (27) presented as an attractive couple. They were married for two years and entered therapy six months after the birth of their first child, a boy. Jim initially called for the consultation, stating how Carol might be having an affair; his repeated demands for a full confession had gone unheeded. He felt the marriage was in big trouble, and he was losing his mind with worry she did not love him anymore. Sexual passion and attractiveness characterized the couple's courtship and first two years of marriage. Each spouse was educated and employed in their respective professions. External family ties were strained, and the couple stated that they were their own family.

During the initial sessions, the couple seemed lost, unhinged by Jim's current suspicions of infidelity, arguing in a way that kept up the heat that Carol should carry the entire responsibility for the falling away of the powerful and passionate love they agreed was initially shared. My balance of empathy and curiosity provided a temporary holding environment, and the couple story unfolded. The predominance of romantic passion reminded me of Fairbairn's idea of the "exciting object" (i.e., a libidinal tie that involves a "forever fantasy" of repairing the broken promise of an infant-parent merger; the fantasy is narcissistically motivated by early intense but later lost love). Each spouse had such a history of being overvalued for attractiveness and cooperativeness, but at a great price—not being loved for oneself. The other striking issue was the birth of a new sibling in each spouse's early childhood and the synchronicity between the intense unconscious mutual feelings of emotional abandonment as a youngster, now repeated with their new son's birth.

Carol painfully admitted ambivalence that her new "love affair" with their son was unexpectedly delicious, because he was un-planned, and that she was also carrying a fear that Jim did not find her as alluring after the birth. She had sought telephone support from the husband of one of her closest friends, and had not in-formed Jim of this, which Jim discovered and took to mean that they were becoming romantically involved. Although Carol's tele-phone contacts sounded "innocent," I thought that she was acting out the ambivalence of (1) guilt over found love for her son, and (2) fear of losing Jim's love. Jim felt unbearable jealousy over the considerable attention Carol paid to their son. He recalled how his younger brother received much of the attention during childhood, and Jim was expected to take care of himself and not need parent-ing. The passion in the courtship and the couple's togetherness had been so reassuring to both spouses in the first two years of the marriage. Later on, however, it backfired. Their merger fantasy was challenged by the unplanned pregnancy, birth, and dependency needs of their infant.

During the six-month treatment process, they disclosed all the disappointments, and spousal miscalculations that were based on basic-assumption thinking (rigid ideas about self and other). The spouses mourned their lost objects, by affectively sharing sadness and resentment concerning childhood-based failures that had over-determined their unconscious motives for fusion.

Successful treatment of the wished-for marriage required attention to deep early losses of "special child" status in each spouse, and promoting self-other differentiation in the current relationship. Work was accomplished in refocusing on the important contributions of otherness in the marriage and family. Marital satisfaction improved when replaced by an acceptance that sexual excitement is no substitute for mature love.

The Defensive Marriage

In the first type of marriage, I described the wished-for marriage model. I emphasized romantic-narcissistic illusions in couples who are tied together by exciting object experiences. These couples are driven by unrealistic expectations of gratification and react to frustrations with regression that leads to disturbed behavior and despair.

In this second example, I present the defensive marriage, which is characterized by a predominance of blocking. *Blocking* is a multilayered couple phenomenon; first consisting of one spouse's blaming, shaming, and trying in earnest to impart marital difficulties as the other spouse's problem. It is easy to assume that when the accused spouse responds passively, he or she *is* the one at fault, which fosters a countertransference of colluding with the aggrieved spouse. In fact, while appearing passive, the accused spouse is internally fuming, but simultaneously allowing all the anger and frustration in the marriage to be carried by the persecuting spouse.

There is, however, a deeper shared unconscious second layer of defense, one more problematic and difficult to engage, because the barrage of hurts and criticisms envelops the space and reduces the therapist's capacity for inquiry. This second layer of the defensive couple concerns a collusion not to reveal the marital underbelly, the more immature individual issues. Intellectualizing, rationalizing, manic behavior, passing the buck, withdrawal, avoidance, denial, and superficial apologies are common defenses of these spouses to detour away from deeper matters.

When the therapist attempts to determine links between marital dissatisfactions and developmental deficits, the couple-as-a-unit oscillates between a cooperative willingness to explore and "going blank." The collusion is engineered to ensure staying together, while bringing some trouble (children, the spouse's ineptitudes, in-laws, the boss, etc.) to the treatment setting. Often the therapist attempts to delve into the means these couples use to avoid dealing with the stated problems. Unfortunately, directly confronting the couple accomplishes little because of their lack of psychological mindedness. Typically the couple offers a weak apology or references external interferences that prevent progress. Spouses placate each other when addressing differences. Underlying these defenses, are unconscious fears of fragmentation or dissolution of the marriage bond if aggression surfaces in both partners. The therapist is relegated to the role of a striving but essentially impotent helper, much in keeping with the couple's projective identificatory system, in which each spouse alternates between the roles of "goodwill ambassador" and "foot dragger." As the therapist silently becomes angrier at the status quo, countertransference awareness can alert him or her that this affect is what the couple fears. Further reflection on one's countertransference can reveal the couple's parallel process in which the therapist also feels like an avoider or "stupid object."

The couple may be also be defending against sadness and vulnerability associated with fear of independent thinking itself. Defenses abound in marital therapy, but the distinction I am making is that couples who unconsciously defend "together" (e.g., "collude") constitute a separate category. Defensive couples project group defenses that overwhelm the therapist. A choice point may be reached when some therapists cannot contain the unconscious collusive aspects, thus losing patience, and the therapist divides the couple into two separate cases; each spouse receives individual therapy with the therapist. When a therapist "acts out" it means the therapist is no longer observing the process, and is disturbed to the extent that the "more difficult spouse" is farmed out to a colleague, and the therapist keeps one spouse with whom he or she is in collusion as the preferred patient. Splitting the couple into separate cases stems from counter-resistance (resistance of the therapist), in contrast with a flexible approach, where offering some individual therapy might be helpful in breaking an impasse.

Case Example

Irene (57) and Ed (66) came to treatment after many years of individual and some marital work in which each of their three children, in succession, had been the focal point of the previous therapies. The child focus that each therapist initially took occurred without the presence of any children in the therapy; this focus had done little to alleviate the children's symptoms or improve the parents' abilities to work together, although they stated they were, in principle, on the same page. An astounding fact emerged: their therapies had totaled twenty years, and each of three therapists had discharged the spouses for lack of progress. Their twenty-year-old daughter, Eve (the last child), had been a perfect student until her senior year of high school, when her grades declined, and she started to stay out late and drink with unsavory characters. Subsequently, Eve flunked out of two colleges and was currently on probation for petty theft and wrecking two cars (DUIs). As she was back at home, the couple was forced to seek help yet again.

The couple started out with a child focus but soon demonstrated a striking inability to work in understanding or shifting their approaches to Eve. Their deeper issues revealed a powerful undertow of rivalry and unstated resentment between Ed and Irene, which they projected onto Eve. Irene projected onto Eve the anger and directness she feared expressing to Ed. Each spouse exhibited displacement. Ed was sweet, gentle, and empathic toward Eve, but she exploited him at every opportunity; yet he held to his approach. Irene was confrontational and intrusive, she tried to discipline and micromanage Eve, who usually tried to cut her off and maintain her distance. Often the therapist identifies with the family situation in feeling that he or she can neither engage nor let go. Coming in touch with this powerful pull into the family dynamic opens a pathway for thinking through the impasse.

The approach I used was to ascertain first what had failed in the previous treatments. At my prompting, we discussed their theories about how the previous therapists failed them. I also raised the possibility of whether an invisible force was preventing a combined effort. I put the phrase in as nonjudgmental a tone as possible and hoped that discussing others' failures might make this subject (the idea of an invisible resistance) less toxic. I silently marveled that after twenty years of therapies, neither spouse could admit any feelings of failure or helplessness. I was also amazed that neither spouse could accuse the other of any faults.

Soon after I offered the suggestion of the possibility that an invisible force was operating, Irene considered quitting therapy. Ed, however, remembered an idea I had shared that unacknowledged fear was behind their respective approaches to Eve. Their very different approaches polarized them and alienated Eve. Ed insisted they continue sessions, and Irene went along. I determined that their previous therapies had been pragmatic and were probably loaded with "how to" techniques. The couple had not explored historically relevant material, for example, how the spouses were carrying their respective parents-of-origin's legacy of childrearing. In contrast to the previous therapists, I offered a historical approach to helping them, resisting the temptation to remain child focused. I would see what we could do together about their mess. I told them they were welcome to bring Eve in for some family work; they reflexively declined.

Over several months, the couple explored life situations that offered a deeper affective experience, one each could relate to (in light of the failures they carried) but had denied responsibility for. They threatened to quit therapy several times, and I told them that was their choice; each time they smiled at my largesse and said they would give *me* another chance. The collusive aspects eventually surfaced, and they were able to admit the denied aggression between them. As they began to feel safer, this allowed them to begin to argue. Though each maintained previous aspects of relating, they were more direct with each other, they admitted mistakes, and I observed less fear of confronting each other about what did and did not work. Eve, who never attended sessions began to calm down, her acting out lessened, and she sought a twelve-step program. Eve had benefited indirectly from the parents' therapy.

Conclusion

The defensive marriage is a category of couple relating that requires special tact and imagination. Although most couples in treatment present some defenses, and we respect and work sensitively with them, defensive couples radiate special collusive aspects that wear therapists out. If we inaccurately assume we are dealing with neurotic anxieties, we may create early impasses. Instead, character traits are at the root of these spouses' personalities (multiplied by two), and the work concerns recognizing the ways that mutual, primitive, unconscious anxieties maintain the relationship while preventing couple and family development. In the defensive marriage, togetherness (couple extreme reliance on coherence) prevails over all else. This marital model requires that we wrestle with considerable disturbance; however, with comprehension of the deep underlying threats of annihilation to these couples, therapy may affect change.

The Split-Off Marriage

Splitting couples give therapists "splitting headaches." We might wonder the reason for a category on splitting. Splitting is a defense to be sure. However, we want to give splitting a special place among the types of couples we encounter, because it is different from other defenses, and as such has unique effects on the couple and the therapist. The most primitive uses of projective identification occur with splitting.

Splitting is unlike most other defenses in that it can represent a long-term severe alteration of external reality. In marriage, each partner carries a different aspect of what the other cannot tolerate. The couple participates in a ritual dance in which disavowed unconscious aspects of the self are projected into the other. An example of splitting occurs when the wife has chosen a husband who is schizoid but who on the surface appears to have the stability, logic, predictability, and consistency that she needs to offset her emotional variability, mood swings, and penchant for excitement. The husband has chosen a wife who offsets his withdrawal from emotion and from human relationships. She functions as a psychological dialysis machine pumping him up and keeping him alive. In this example of a couple's projective matrix, we can see how fragile couples use aspects of each other's personalities to make up for what each is missing—a whole self. In the course of the relationship, the rigid part-object constellation will undergo the test of time and strain on the partners.

Severe splitting may consist of unconscious infantile wishes of a sexual, aggressive, or autonomy-dependency quality that are loaded with conflict and rejected within the self. Preoedipal part-object relations are split off from consciousness. These part-object experiences stem from deprivation scenarios from each spouse's childhood. For example, in some marriages, each spouse is preoccupied with raging unconscious Oedipal rivalry. Whatever the origins, the couple has an unconscious valency to maintain rigid object relations that interfere with pleasurable development and sharing. The splitting mechanism serves to maintain a pathological equilibrium of a deeply disturbed type. Borderline-schizoid marriages (McCormack, 2000) personify a frequency of splitting that polarizes spouses in anger or despair, unable to recognize the deeper conflicts generating the distress. These couples fear either fragmentation through fusion or the alternate fear of losing oneself in the other. Spousal fears of loss of cohesiveness evolve from basic internal developmental failures. Spouses with such fears may fluctuate between intense dependencies and intense flight from dependency. Autonomy can be subverted by pseudo-independence when a spouse takes flight from dependency, which prevents sharing oneself with another. These problems may result in accusations of unreliability by both partners. Couples maintain rigid positions, which usually indicate massive splitting. This defense plagues marital work and is most challenging to the capacity of the therapist to manage the affects associated with primitive spousal anxieties.

A clinical feature of splitting is that the couple therapist can be split by the couple. One spouse finds him or her competent and idealizes the possibilities of being understood, meaning that this spouse's point of view about the marriage will be supported. The other spouse views the therapist with mistrust and disdain, expecting to do battle with his or her every observation or intervention.

Immediately the therapist is faced with a potential impasse early the treatment. Who does the therapist represent, and how does the therapist engage the couple when placed in an impossible situation?

The Clinical Situation

In one such situation I was faced with being idealized and denigrated by a couple that presented their problem as a waning sexual appetite. At first, I found them attractive and was drawn to their physical appearance, with a slight feeling of envy, then I experienced them as insatiable; being idealized by the wife, I felt the pressure to give in to her, and with the husband, I felt I could never win his trust. Using these feelings led to imagining what the inside of the spousal relationship might be about as I considered the waning of their sexual relationship. Each spouse had projected into me the split-off part of what they could not negotiate with the other. There was no awareness of an unconscious relationship, which was most important to informing their troubled situation. I was carrying the unknown parts while trying to make contact with each of them in a way they could take in. From the information I received, a few speculations came to mind about their dynamics. The wife's disowned part involved the expectation that a husband should meet her every need, mind-reading included (the therapist's), while she would serve him as a maternal figure—domestic perfection, social secretary, bookkeeper, and support person. The husband projected his mistrust of the maternal function (the therapist) that he also relied on, fearing being engulfed by it, hence an infantile fear of fusion/merger. The wife and husband had a rather naïve approach to the complexities inherent in building a marriage and were quite stuck. The physical attractiveness (which I had initially been drawn to) appeared to be the basis for their bonding, and their growing unconscious anxieties about infantile symbiotic ties and terrors, threatened the sexual relationship that held them together.

With a few ideas to balance me, I decided to verbalize their respective uses of me in order to open a space for us to consider how that could relate to their impasse and underlying issues. I found a moment when each was doing the customary splitting—he ignoring my input, with disdain, and she taking in my every word as nectar (milk) from the gods (breast). I pointed out how they viewed our relationship in these contrasting ways, which kept part of me for each of them, representing something to long for (in the wife) and something to turn away from (in the husband). My aim was to determine the couple's capacity for locating their split-off dependency conflicts by showing how alive these were in the treatment relationship (transferences).

After some silence, the husband took the opportunity by expressing a good amount of irritation of his spouse's high expectations of me. He was identifying with me in the role in which he was becoming more and more uncomfortable at home. His ambivalence came through, in that he wanted her to do more to water their sexual drought but admitted that the reduction of sexual relations offered some relief for him. She joined in, stating that her high expectations of him covered over a fear that he did not love her. The splitting momentarily lifted, revealing the spouses' beginning capacity to venture into the core territory of unconscious relations.

The splitting couple presents concrete thinking and behavior and rigid character traits. Understanding the splitting process requires attention to detail about the way in which unconscious psychic process restricts the marriage and replays in the marital therapy. In practice, the splitting of the therapist's ego allows an experiencing of the representations of each spouse's split-off parts; this acceptance can inform us as to the couple's compromise formation. As in the previous two types of marriage, I re-emphasize that countertransference analysis offers insights into the internal world of each couple and the impact of transferences on the work to be accomplished.

The work with these three couples focused on countertransference analysis as it informed my understanding of underlying dynamics that were impeding progress. The last couple sufficiently resolved their split to trust the treatment. When losing my way (inability to comprehend couple and couple-therapist transferences), unconscious resonances shook up the unintegrated split off parts of the projective system that had blocked the space for thinking; a new opening provided adjustments in my communications. Creation of new safety and mending of the splits emerge from unconscious sensibility as to how the partners functioned within the treatment triangle and, most importantly, what the therapist represented (e.g., persecutor, lover, intruder, merger-symbiotic partner). In real terms, I had to re-work the splits inside me before the couple's impasse could be addressed. In these cases, an in-depth approach was needed, given the degree of pathological relating. In the last case, the extreme splitting penetrated my mind, causing an enactment that was preventing the couple from working through their difficulties. In-depth work is essential when chaos and extreme differences prevent the couple from arriving at a common goal. Projective identification in couple cases require the therapist's use of countertransference to learn what emotions are being projectively identified into him, as they are most certainly at the root of disturbed relating. Rational approaches and advice-giving will fall flat because the couple lacks basic organization around mutual needs and wants. Until the therapist finds an opening where the soft underbelly of wounded couples can be addressed, aggression and despair most certainly will prevail.

Chapter Five

Couple Assessment and Treatment of Narcissistic Anxieties and Defenses

Narcissism is not a fact; it is a clinical entity!

One of the most difficult treatment entities, particularly in couple work, is malignant narcissism. Narcissistic self-involvement threatens any treatment due to difficulty in permitting a trusted dependency and a positive transference with the therapist. It is important to apply our in-depth treatment of partnerships to relationships that have at least one narcissist. Our theory holds fast to the notion that is takes two to construct a personal relationship, and projective identification is a two-person phenomenon, even when one partner has a narcissistic personality.

Healthy narcissism is about individuality and a self that is cohesive and sustainable over time and that continues through developmental pathways and the life cycle. A cohesive self produces an idiom in a voice that reinforces the "I". The variability of a life lived with others alters earlier naïve childhood perspectives on self-cohesion and ensures adaptability. Adaptation and self-cohesion require that early experiences were reasonably secure. From an interpersonal perspective, when the child is *self-confident* throughout early development, we would assume that he or she has been accepted by the primary caregivers; thus the true self is at hand, and the "I-Thou" potential is balanced, allowing the other to be a self (separate whole object) as well. Uniqueness and consistency accompany the self on its travels and in encounters with trials and tribulations, but the self not only endures, it is shaped anew. Optimally the self is not taken hostage by experience. Hence a self that feels confident in its identity and complexities has its roots in healthy narcissism. Much of our healthy narcissism is derived on the basis of the freedom to explore the world with safety, to express emotion without retaliation, and to experience life's frustrations and losses with reliable others who help us to process our feelings.

A narcissistically secure self is secure by the luck and good grace of its connections to others. The security needed for coherence and continuity is dependent on how well an individual is received, nurtured and individualized by family and culture. Interpersonal competence in adult life depends on resilience in those whose narcissistic investments in the child were justified. When the child lives to please others, however, development becomes overdetermined by internalized and rigid demands for compliance. Hence, resilience is lacking in later life. Uncomplicated narcissism is balanced by how well the baby satisfied parental psychological aims while retaining a separate integrated self.

Was there a sufficient space where a child could thrive? What about the pairings, personalities, and capacities of the caregivers responsible for attending to the child's needs? Optimally children successfully negotiate the oedipal period, accept that their parents sleep together and have an exclusive relationship separate from the child. They can recover when parents manage their marital needs without placing undue pressure on the child to make up for a spouse's deficits. The well-balanced child has handled the intrusion and delight of siblings, experienced deaths of their elders, and profited from the challenges of ordinary life.

Children need an emotional "immune system" that protects them from trauma and external deficiencies, such as when maturational or developmental capabilities do not match the expectations of the caregiver. For children with a difficult infancy, ordinary love might be insufficient to mitigate the wounding of the child. Limitations in bonding became fueled by a problem with the "fit" after an initial period of parental adoration, possibly followed by preference for a new sibling. The shadow of having been rejected leads to a preoccupation with regaining lost status. Future bonding experiences are held hostage to what was lost and (unless there is a new discovery of what was lost) are accompanied by the pain of recognition and regret that a renewed hope for improved bonding will not be achieved. An entitlement stirred by emptiness, fueled by tyranny to being served with no chance of mutuality, will likely get repeated.

NARCISSISM AND THE COUPLE

Based on the previous description of narcissism, adult pairings inevitably become replicas of failed early ones. Mate selection is especially precarious if motives are fashioned by infantile fantasies of being saved or served by the other. In this scenario, Freud viewed narcissistic love as "A person may love—or treat or sculpt another." According to the anaclitic attachment type: "a. A woman who feeds him, b. A man who protects him" (Freud, 1914, *On Narcissism*, SE, vol. XIV, p. 90). The therapeutic action of psychoanalysis is based on Freud's metaphor that we try to free the sculptor from the stone.

Jeremy Holmes (*The Search for a Secure Base*, 2001) describes the narcissistic dilemma:

> Here conflict is between the narcissism of an organism determined to maximize evolutionary fitness in the short term, and the long-term need for collaboration, which means the ability to

put purely selfish aims to one side when necessary and to value
relatedness. Being able to understand another's point of view is
an essential part of this process, as is the ability to see oneself
and one's desires from the outside. (p. 27)

Holmes's language favors neo-Darwinism on the origins of intrapsychic conflict, in keeping with a Freudian tradition. He captures
the essential core of the problem of narcissistic personalities—they
are unable to get past an encapsulated version of the self in relation
to internalized objects. As fractured as the borderline structure is
(Lachkar, 1992), which makes for frailty and severe emotional
fluctuation, the narcissistic core consists of a distinct self, with
grandiosity and glorified self representations, loaded with self-cer-
tainty and clamoring for a devoted audience.

Narcissistic tendencies may fluctuate within the same individual
or operate as distinctive tendencies projected between the partners.
For example, there is the clinging narcissist, who colonizes through
entitlement. This mode consists of the demand to be indulged by
selfless care and is a distinct style. The self-insulated over-individ-
uated partner is somewhat different. Self-sufficient and always correct, they create conflict in the other partner due to distancing with
a partner who requires dependency to feel connected. While feast-
ing on a self-assurance established by independence and certainty,
there is nonetheless a contradiction: the rigid certainty that one's
view is the only view results from splitting of the self. The demand
for a cloning experience exhorts the other partner to be "attuned" at
all times. This requirement presses partners into obligations rather
than an affective nonverbal resonance, which is useful in therapy
when used empathically.

In therapy, attunement subjectively recasts an interpersonal experience into another form of expression via the transference; the
transference experience functions automatically and is less cognitive but is similar to the original child experiences in timing, intensity, and shape. Transference differentiates those dependencies

emerging from relatively benign entitlement derived from prior exposure to reliable dependency from neglected or misshapen ones. When narcissistic parents foster excessive dependency beyond childhood, they ensure that others are taken for granted and exploited, and there is little accountability for what is received. This type of narcissism ensnares the other partner in the dance of usury.

The mother who is empathically attuned preserves the baby's inner states, while offering an emotional connection toward eventual symbolic meaning-making through interpersonal comfort (Stern, 1985). Not so with obsessive narcissists due to the inordinate demand for like-mindedness in the partner. Agreement by force field characterizes the demand for cloning.

Narcissistic entitlements are systemic in that interpersonal relations must adhere to pre-emptive beliefs; optimal satisfaction stems from one-sided preoccupations with pumping up self-esteem, by co-opting the other to provide. This excessive use of the other is for adoration, the loving eternal gaze, and other services. Demands from a narcissistic partner can be satisfied only if the other sacrifices their autonomy. "I feel, therefore I act" typifies the narcissistic motives. Development is frozen at a level requiring repetition, sameness, and consistency. The result is house of cards, in which entitlements reinforce one's sense of self—a treasure of endless devotion by the recipient partner is thick with thorns, illustrated during courtship as the giving partner extends the very interest and seductive attentiveness required to match up with the needs of the narcissist. However, the dance is destined to be short-lived due to the inevitable expectation of the reverse—"You give, I take."

The giving partner has a reciprocal problem in development. By giving without faltering, the phantasy is that love will result as long as the lead is taken and repeated. The narcissistic partner may possess charm, courtship skills, and apparent confidence; those qualities are lacking in the giving partner and are attractive and compelling motives to live up to the rigid expectations that will keep the narcissist interested.

To restate, two types of entitlement are (1) the right to chronic emotional restoration (e.g., "I have suffered"), and (2) "I am strong, yet I can demand a privilege of forced satisfaction," as in likemindedness. Availability of the other is by demand, with a likely discounting of guilt over treating others poorly.

GETTING THE NARCISSIST'S ATTENTION IN COUPLE THERAPY

The following are two features of malignant narcissism:

1. The illusion of self-sufficiency.
2. The expectation of an unreliable dependency.

Technical Approach to Reaching the Narcissistic Relationship

We work with the non-narcissistic parts and the depressive-position potential (Klein, 1946).

We look for commonalities with the spouse and speculate on the danger of feeling the conflict of togetherness *and* separateness.

We prefer language that shows curiosity not certainty.

We preserve each spouse's self.

We titrate the potential for accepting another's viewpoint, through gradual therapeutic communication.

We point to the co-existence of conflicting motives.

We promote awareness of thwarted dependency aims.

We use language that offers alternate explanations for the concrete.

We offer unsaturated interpretations, on here and now issues, leaving the distant past until much later, when trust is available.

We contain the projections.

We introduce the language of love and hate as two parts of a relationship.

We acknowledge what each spouse believes.

We ask about dangerous desires.

We reframe the icing-up of relationships by excessive predictability and perfectionism.

We comment on levels of suffering.

We mentalize narcissistic terror and recognize that the need for nourishment from another that cannot be controlled by the self is most feared because it reduces the narcissist's fragile image of complete independence.

Narcissus myth: Narcissus is trapped, gazing at something he subjectively believes is a lost loved object, but is objectively the idealized aspect of his own self. He believes himself to be in love. He dies of starvation, however, because he cannot turn toward a real object from which he might have been able to get what he really needed. Entitlement forgives debt by eliminating its place in loss and of having to experience grief.

While on the topic of narcissistic pathology, let's include the narcissistic motives of the therapist, whose self-awareness of personal valences influences treatment.

THERAPIST ENTITLEMENTS: BASIC ASSUMPTIONS OF WELL-MEANING THERAPISTS

Therapists generally expect the following:

1. A relatively engaging working alliance (cooperative patients from the outset).

2. Interpretive prerogatives (patients will take them in with appreciation).
3. Patients want to change (why else would they come to and pay for therapy?).
4. Positive transference (they like us because we are lovable and kind).
5. Couples will come as long as therapy is needed (they are patient, and they want to give us as much time as we need).

Narcissism in marriage and in couple therapy involves benign to malignant manifestations of two individuals' epicenters fueled by unconscious motives for mate selection from courtship on. Whatever the couple's fit, the therapist will observe it from the first telephone contact. An encounter with severe narcissistic tendencies entails containing toxic intrusions within the dance of two personalities that at first appear to have nothing in common. The overlap of couple personalities ranges from borderline, schizoid, histrionic, obsessive-compulsive to depressive. In the course of therapy, the couple may initially present with one manifestation of their fit, as in a polarized disagreement concerning a trivial matter. How does a couple reconcile polarized complaints, and how do they reconcile completely different versions of the partner or self?

The dominant organizing principle for impasse is *disorganized couple identity*—reciprocal interactions that mutually rebuff, disappoint or degrade one's longings—each partner invalidates the other's need to be understood so that neither can modulate, contain or ameliorate one's disruptive affective state. The marital bond is under siege, so the beleaguered partner assumes any candid discussion threatens the other partner's identity. There are enactments of unconscious disturbances, and the partner's exterior defenses take over against anxiety. We call this merger of personalities a *folie a deux*!

The following vignette illustrates couple preoccupations with narcissistic aims. A madness of two minds interacting (*folie a deux*) can be illustrated by a couple separated for eleven months and living in two different countries with their two young children, an eighteen-month-old girl and a two-and-a-half-year-old boy living with the mother and her family. Litigation over the taking of the children from one country to another without the father's consent had made it impossible for the couple to meet and discuss the marriage, or for the father to see the children in person, because there were arrest warrants on him should he come to the wife's family residence. Her family was involved in the punitive approach. He saw the children on Skype.

At the eleventh month of the unworkable arrangement, the couple met in New York on their own, and they sought treatment to determine if reconciliation might be possible. The legal claims had been harsh and destructive, with one partner blaming the other for kidnapping, and the other partner claiming assault. During a series of exploratory sessions, the couple admitted meeting secretly (family members and lawyers did not know of the meeting) for two days to hammer out a postnuptial agreement on custody and visitation if they could not reconcile. They had addressed the destructive results of the hasty separation of almost one year and were able to arrive at an agreement, which the wife wrote down. They discussed the arrangement on the way to the session that morning, and there was a breakdown in thinking and conversing about the facts and expectations concerning the children's summers.

The wife had become unnerved and distraught, unable to consent to what the husband claimed was the agreed-upon summer schedule in which he would have both children for the entire summer, she would have a one-week vacation with them during that time, and there would be a few preparation days with mother before the children's trip to his home country where his family lived; a few days before fall began, the mother would have a re-entry period with the children (custodial parent nine months of the year).

The more the husband reminded the wife of the specific days agreed upon in writing, the less the wife could accept them. The *folie a deux* emerged as he insisted or bullied her with facts, and she unraveled and grew more and more terrified. She threatened to leave the room, and I had my hands full in calming them enough to think about the impossible situation they were in. I told them he was afraid of trickery, so the facts were his best means of security after eleven months apart from his children. He was worried he would lose access to them in the future. I told her that she could not agree to the arrangement because any adherence to a strict arrangement would feel like he was still controlling her as in the claustrophobic marriage from which she fled. I also said firmly that the children's needs for both parents had been least considered in their deliberations, and we had better work on that before they signed on to strict arrangements. In due time, they calmed, and the basic mistrust issues were amplified, with the result that they reworked the agreement and we continued to discuss how the relationship had deteriorated to drive them so mad.

Underlying Process

Discrete and discontinuous internal states of mind construct fixed and concrete ideas. We access these through observing the transferences; oscillations vary between restrictive to confused meanings of complex motives and behaviors. In the partners' fit, there may be too much conscious anxiety or too little anxiety in relation to underlying issues (below the surface).

Case Example of Not-So-Trivial Pursuits

Early in the assessment phase, Marge and Dan were polarized in their constant fighting over their different approaches to family relations. Marge's mom recently had severe lower back pain and got Marge (a physician) to write her a Vicodin prescription. Three days passed since the onset of the pain, yet she insisted on attending Marge and Dan's eight-year-old's birthday party. Barely able to move, she needed help to get to the bathroom. Marge's explanation when Dan asked why she hadn't gone to the emergency room when in such severe pain was that mother was waiting three days to see her own physician. Dan's position was that Marge's family regularly seeks each other out, and this takes over Marge's time and focus. Marge's angry retort was that Dan's mother had knee surgery a week ago, and Marge had been in touch, but Dan had not. Marge felt Dan was not caring enough to look in on his mom, leaving her to do it. Dan's response was that he was in touch with his dad, and his mom had left instructions not to be called while in rehab.

Each spouse's family represents a culture that requires adherence to rules of engagement that the couple is unable to negotiate together. We have enmeshment on Marge's side and strict boundaries on Dan's side. The two sides are acceptable to them as individuals because they view their family relations as ordinary. When I experienced their couple strife, the combined differences appeared similar. They were operating in an unquestioned rigid set of family relating that, I inferred, represented a repetition of childhood attachments. The partners were caught up in anger that was blinding them to other possibilities. Skepticism fueled doubts disguised as defensive rebuttals. What was presumed right for one, caused rejection and hurt to the other, partly due to unquestioned parts of each partner's sacrifice at the altar of family loyalty. Couple loyalty was under siege.

My response to their narcissistic hurts was to offer that hurt was beneath the surface of their angry exchanges. Neither one had thought to question on their own what the partner was now anxiously challenging. Each was holding on tight to one way of dealing with family matters and the hurt was growing. I thought they each had a tight set of family allegiances that they strongly defended against, and that was keeping their couple needs at a standstill. What I offered was a way of thinking about their firmly held alliances to individual family cultures that unconsciously kept defeating any possibility (or avenue) of being a creative couple.

Depending on the therapist's personality and interventions, we may see individual and couple fluctuations from the autistic-contiguous to P/S to depressive position (Ogden, 1982). The goal of therapy with narcissistic vulnerability is to transform the more toxic renditions into usable and palatable language. Any position held by the therapist will be challenged due to the problem of containment inherent in narcissistic vulnerability. Theoretically the psychic world is fused to the interpersonal in a *folie a deux*, so that the therapist is expected to hold the same views as the narcissistic partner. When a container is offered by the therapist, the narcissistic partner may be able to receive but not give. By fusion or collusion, the couple and the therapist are faced with "K" (attack on knowledge) and "C" (rejection of curiosity) defenses. Attacks on linking (Bion, 1963) involve defenses consisting of a numbing of thought, and dissociation or fear of losing one's mind. The idea of "K" refers to Bion's notion that concrete knowledge disallows new thinking, so that opening up space for new ideas (K) or interpretations is met with rigid defenses. Curiosity is basic to creative thinking but requires a relaxing of adhesive ideas, so that I refer to "C" as an unconscious or conscious attack on curiosity. Any opening for an exploration of meaning is threatening to what is already "known," so a couple will eject ideas, thoughts, or attempts at understanding as foreign to survival.

DISSOCIATION ILLUSTRATED

Dissociation is a fundamental organizer of personality organization and a defensive shaper of the interpersonal world. Dissociation is a mind-body encapsulation that embodies an absence of dialectical thinking and perceiving. Dissociation anesthetizes and isolates mental pain. It functions as a self-hypnotic process. Distancing the mind from the sensory apparatus, it operates as a defensive organization of mental structure, preventing the symbolizing of experience, resulting in an absence of authenticity. The mind flees its subjectivity and evacuates pain associated with the emotional exposure to internal truth (bad objects).

Unlinked domains of the self include the de-repressed or traumatized parts; the psyche-soma is reduced to physical suffering, with ailments that are difficult to medically diagnose; the libido is in a flight from the anguish of psychic conflict; pseudo vitality or pseudo gratification results, as in manic or compulsive activity (exercise or longer work hours) and there is no resolution of narcissistic wounds. The smoothness of the defensive system covers over the dissociative one, in which repetition, not discovery, is the aim. The narcissistic cocoon represents pseudo-integration, an illusion of self-sufficiency in a world of resource less dependency.

An example of dissociative driven motives involves the love of sports in a forty-three-year-married stock broker who would rather play hockey, golf, and basketball with male buddies than be with his long-suffering accommodating wife. This is a case of stuck meaning-driven behavior.

A forced, ritualized, and repetitively concrete meaning to his behavior evacuated any new possibilities or discoveries of other meanings for his presumed love of sports. An illusion of simplistic meaning accompanied all early discussions, although he came for therapy because he was becoming aware he *might* be selfish. A forced adherence to established meanings enables the self to coerce inauthentic parts, dissociated from memory, in a fixed self perspective, to force the environment—in this case, a wife and three children, who hungered for the attention of a father/husband—to go along. The husband's misappropriation of libido (false self) is a counterfeit defensive expression of "staying alive" without living or relating. Dissociation prevents new information and perspectives from entering the mind so that the patient is insulated and isolated from new experiences.

Paradoxically, should there be a tampering with the patient's usual means of expression (the somatic aspect, in a premature attempt at less physical recreation), in favor of more home life, a flood of unmetabolized feeling may emerge, with attendant fragmentation. If there is an interference with the patient's usual means of expression as in an emerging memory of mother's marked indifference to the patient as a child during violent outbursts by the father, more sensory aliveness might emerge, with attendant disturbance.

Dissociation results in an on-alert pseudo-aliveness that keeps psychic deadness under the radar. As such, the compulsive search for self-validation is a clue to the treatment of narcissistic disorders. Beneath the action-oriented pursuits is deeper dread that life is passing one by. There may be a dim awareness in the couple that the existential deadness will not prevent loss. The loss may be signaled by the partner's wish to be free of the narcissist.

Therapist Technical Moves When Faced with Withdrawal or Detachment

Withdrawal versus Detachment

Detachment is the more serious defense, as the person loses the libidinal attachment to an object, as in a split-off despondency. Withdrawal is a midpoint in which some investment remains. Intervening with detachment involves acknowledging that an event is occurring in which a partner needs to withdraw inside the self. Can the detached partner locate him/herself? With withdrawal, we ask what is occurring in the room that might be uncomfortable (words that are less threatening) or disruptive, so as to lose interest in the session or treatment. The level of patient interiority requires a proper language for location of hidden anxiety. We do not ask the partner why they are not paying attention. When encountering the more regressive internal experience of detachment, we initially steer away from confrontational language about the nature of the internal mental state that threatens—for example, we can tactfully address what is inside the room but just outside the partner's deepest dread. We can mention the therapist's and other partner's relationship and so forth if that is not too intrusive. Therapist style and each circumstance will determine the approach to withdrawal or detachment.

Illustration of Proper Holding Language When Thinking Is Blocked

Ben (64) and Lisa (59) were seeing me in couple therapy for ten months, after Ben had made destructive business decisions without Lisa's knowledge that almost cost them their assets. Deception and poor judgment typified Ben, whose underlying arrogance and sense of entitlement was a long-term narcissistic tendency in which Lisa sacrificed much to remain loyal to him. Doing business his way and making questionable and risky investments eventually backfired, with enormous tax consequences that pressed the couple into working together to prevent a financial-legal catastrophe.

They had been doing a bit better in addressing the reciprocal problems in the long-term marriage underlying the destructive aspects of Ben going down the path to ruin. The couple had reported that their therapy with me was stabilizing their wounded relationship and was opening a space for exploring the deep-rooted anxieties between them. I recommended that Ben increase his individual therapy from one to three times per week (with another therapist). In our next session, he began by reporting that he could not tell his individual therapist that week why I recommended the increase in sessions. He forgot what my reasons were. Ben often asked me directly what he should think, say, and do to assuage Lisa's rage and despair, and so this was consistent with a usual blocking of memory. I did not usually address "how to" questions, except to ask what his thoughts were behind the requests. In this instance, he said he needed to retrieve his glasses to "hear what I was saying," and he stood up, moving to the door, also indicating he wanted a pen and paper so he could write down my answers.

As I heard the words "See what I was saying," I could not avoid a chuckle, noticing his wife was quietly chuckling too. I asked Ben not to leave the room at that moment, as I wanted us to consider his actions as an experience of something to do with me. Ben leaned toward me, wide-eyed, and angrily asked, "Are you laughing at me? Do you think I'm the village fool?" This was the first expression of anger and disturbance I had experienced with him directed toward me. I paused and said I did not think the chuckle was meant at his expense but rather was a response to his previous reference about seeing and hearing through his glasses. He paused and sat down, partly in awe, trying to decide what to do. Lisa chimed in by reminding him that I was the therapist who did not let him get away with things like his current therapist of eighteen years did. She said that Ben did this to her as well when he felt criticized. He would get angry, charging that he was not stupid and would not tolerate being told his faults. I waited for Ben to reply.

Ben said he really was confused between (1) his sudden need to write down what I talked about so he could remember and use it and to talk to his therapist about what we covered, and (2) my general preference that he sit with his feelings and try tuning in to them. I had an idea about the chronic issue of Ben's blocked thinking, so I asked, "Did your parents speak any other languages at home besides English?" Lisa interjected that his mother spoke poorly, and his father would merge two languages (of the three that he spoke) into his sentences. Ben had always been frustrated because he could not communicate with his parents. I asked if he resented or felt ashamed of his parents for their not adapting to his needs and to US culture. He said directly, with bitterness and pain, "I was always ashamed of my parents."

We went on to discuss the details of his family, survivors of the Great Depression, who could not adapt. Lisa added that her family was crazy and self-centered and that she withdrew as much as possible, but her sacrificial tendencies were not left behind, emotionally speaking. At this point, I offered Ben an impression that his shame was complex and went deeper than just the surface feelings about his parents, because he tended to deny it existed. I shared a thought that in our earlier interchange, his anger that I treated him with disdain, like the "village fool," might represent an unacknowledged aspect (as a reversal of roles) of the way his mother felt when Ben got angry with *her* when she did not understand him. This type of projective identification in therapy is called a *complementary transference*. Ben related that mother's childhood in fact took place in a small village where there were no schools. Was Ben the "village fool" in his marriage and unconsciously the angry part of his mother? Ben felt ashamed, but the shame was deeper and more nuanced then he had previously considered. Ben turned the "bad boy" guilt feelings against himself as a consequence of hating the mother on which he relied. He was "ignorant" and turned limited insight into a defensive attack on others. The projective process was now being enacted in the session. We might now make sense of it as it unfolded between us.

I thought about what I was encountering and concluded that Ben had demonstrated the difference between detachment and withdrawal. Detachment required destroying the needed object, having no relationship to it, and relying totally on oneself, which existed as a blocked capacity to think about the ways his self-sabotaging be-havior affected others. No guilt or remorse was needed as long as deeds were repressed or rationalized and deceptions were fully in place. Withdrawal took place in our encounter, as he was invested in me and was able to react to being wounded by my words and affect. His investment in the helping relationship allowed some comprehension of the psychical representations that his enactment brought to my mind. The language I used was reassuring that I meant Ben no harm. We continued the exploration of what histori-cally derived unconscious motives illustrated building material from our encounter.

CONCLUDING THOUGHTS

I have demonstrated features of narcissistic pathology of couples that find a way into the therapist's responsive self. An in-depth approach is needed with cases of severe narcissistic impairment because the limitations in trust are great. Giving therapeutic direc-tion almost always increases rejection or humiliation in the more narcissistically stricken partner. When enactments occur in treat-ment, new material is available that illuminates unconscious anxie-ties about prior relationships that have frozen the couple's capac-ities for authentic experiencing and prevented the providing of a safe holding. Treatment with narcissistically wounded and wound-ing partners takes place in a psychic and interactive space, requir-ing the therapist to locate and empathize with the earlier split-off deficits in family life so that the painful affect associated with the wounding process can surface and losses can be grieved.

A caveat about in-depth approaches in couple therapy with ma-jor narcissistic disorders is that rage, hostility, and despair may accompany the surfacing of dependency's hidden wounds, and the grief underlying their discoveries may not immediately surface—sadomasochistic patterns resulting from the victim and victimizer patterns from the past now reside in the couple relationship, with subtlety or menace. The therapist is hard pressed when attempting to reverse the destructive aspects in these types of partnerships; couple therapy with this population is an arduous and long-term task, given the depth of the original traumas and deficits and the rigidity of defenses against suffering re-injury, often witnessed as self-justifications that accompany sadistic exploitations. As always, therapists are well advised to pay attention to their countertransference because unacknowledged countertransference can turn treatment into a triad of sadomasochistic exchanges.

We have explored facets of narcissistic pairings and have discussed conceptual and technical rationales required in the holding of several treatment couples. These couples manifest deep conflicts within damaged selves. There were no practical solutions for developmental catastrophes. Long-term work can gradually take hold, but pitfalls frequently occur, and building trust, as stated at the outset, feels like quicksand. A final observation on the difficulties encountered with narcissistic pathology concerns the therapist's struggle to remain neutral. Located somewhere between indifference ("We do not care") and detachment ("We are overwhelmed so we mentally flee"), we find *neutrality*. Neutrality entails staying connected to the couple and keeping our heads about us when the partners pressure for side-taking or complete individual loyalty. One technique I use to re-find my lost neutrality (inevitable with very disturbed cases) is to pay attention to the space between the couple, focusing on the in-between communications. No technique is foolproof; however, I find visualization of space between the partners can aid perspective when projective material is being actively launched, received, blocked, and countered. The interpsychic system can co-exist in my mind along with the individual clamoring for attention.

The challenge of working effectively with narcissism in marriage requires an in-depth approach, adapted to the particular defenses and vulnerabilities of couples with narcissistic pathology. Individuals with narcissistic disorders and their long-suffering partners have an unconscious fit that defies simple techniques or a persuasive approach to change. Deep psychic wounds limit these patients and their marriages. Whether the partners are defended by rigidity, invulnerability and haughty independence, or easily rewounded, solicitous for approval, and highly sensitive, the therapist remains poised, hovering between empathy and gentle inquiry; until an opening might be found for a new emotional experience.

Chapter Six

Infidelity and Intimacy

Working with the Extramarital Affair

A PERSPECTIVE ON MONOGAMY AND INFIDELITY

Any discussion of infidelity requires some attention to the historical roots of monogamy and the ways couples respond to internalized culture. We often confuse fidelity with sexual exclusivity retained for marriage. This is not the only way to measure devotion and loyalty in marriage. Monogamy, as a social arrangement, is not a state of mind, per se, or a moral precept, as tradition informs us, and anthropologists question its evolutionary advantages. Historically, we might conjecture that sexual infidelity has been aided by monogamy, in that marriage was historically for one purpose, sex and romance for another. We have a historically derived split! The splitting phenomena in cases of infidelity may have intergenerational or cultural antecedents, and being informed of background influences regarding monogamy must not be overlooked when doing an assessment.

I am distinguishing (1) culturally derived transgenerational values of devotion, loyalty, and fidelity as benefits of monogamy, from (2) issues of sexual exclusivity that reflect society's need for stability in families. Although we would view fidelity in all forms as a virtue, it is much broader and deeper than sexual fidelity. Sexual fidelity is therefore a matter of introjected feelings, intentions, and intensities, and one can be unfaithful and betraying *without* a sexual partner outside of the marriage!

Sexual loyalty is a derivative of romantic notions concerning marriage. Motivations for achieving this are complex and subject to variations in personal backgrounds, gender-based options, religious beliefs, and fluctuating societal sanctions for sexual behavior. We would also include the eventual and inevitable lessening of purely romantic motives for sustaining marriage the longer a marriage lasts, because couples cannot maintain the original heightened physical attraction commensurate with early courtship.

Sexual needs are still important in the marital life cycle. Sexual needs can be enriched, worked on, and modified throughout the life cycle. Marital success over time depends on long-term experiences of living together. Couple and family life cycle issues include childrearing tasks, threats to spousal health, career and financial concerns, external kinship matters, stressors and traumas, losses and way they are dealt with, emotional fluctuations of family members, and intergenerational differentiations of roles and tasks; a variety of situations have to be integrated into the life of the couple. Sex will influence and be influenced by the ways the couple collectively copes with these many important life events and tasks.

CLINICAL DYNAMICS OF INFIDELITY

To say that fidelity is complex is to begin to open our eyes to the broader and deeper meanings of the extramarital affair. I view extramarital affairs as the particular form of acting out, or symptomatic conduct of one spouse (or both) indicative of failed communications and powered by unconscious forces leading to a deficient and counterfeit couple bond. Fidelity, defined as a relationship of emotional and physical bonding in its deepest sense, has been eroded.

The type of infidelity I am referring to may consist of a one-night fling or a long-term love relationship. What either type means to the couple is what we are clinically interested in. As a matter of clinical fact, some couples collude for years in mutual contempt with a dyadic unconscious agreement to ignore extramarital relationships. This is in keeping with the internal object relationships that provide for the "safety of mutual belonging." Acknowledging a breach in the dyadic boundaries would produce the terror and panic of split-off abandonment. Couples in collusion are often part-object related and embody the need to defend against panic of dissolving their dependency at the price of loyalty. An affair can "protect" the couple from hostile or passive dependencies, which, if surfaced, would signal deeper emotional or sexual conflicts within and between the spouses. The affair could symbolically reflect "secret" longings that are too frightening to admit to with one's mate, but when they are shared with another, or even in fantasy, an aspect of the marriage can be retained (a pseudo wholeness) by use of the *third object* (this term is distinct from the "analytic third," which refers to the combined therapist-patient mentalization that results in insight and transformation). Retaliatory fears can also heighten the excitement of the affair with the secret dependencies on the brink of discovery and punishment (shame). One spouse can have a companion set of longings, acted out by (projective identified into) the other spouse, while the more contained spouse fantasizes, fears, and slow boils with suspicion. Another tragic feature of an affair is that the spouse participating in it can no longer be spontaneous or authentic in the marriage.

An important couple dynamic with infidelity is that couples oscillate between separation fears and autonomy fears (fission-fusion). The affairee (the person with whom a spouse has an affair) can be a stabilizer, allowing the marriage some basis for continuity. Needs are being met in the triangle so that the couple dyad does not have to seriously address marital conflicts. Affairs usually do not end the relationship; they are a catalyst in dramatizing the missing links in the marital relationship. In other instances, an affair signals the ending effort of one or the other spouse, or a final "nail" in the coffin of an almost dead marriage that no one wants to bury. Such is the power of feared endings. The affair is then used as a transitional relationship by a spouse who may eventually make the affairee spouse number two, three, or four. At times, a love relationship may be developing but within the still-existing dead marriage, so the marriage is betrayed in order to set up a tragedy so great, due to the guilt in the "infidel," the more symbiotic and clinging partner allows the infidel to leave (actually, to be thrown out).

A dimension of infidelity that receives too little attention is a perverse pairing involving one spouse in long-term individual therapy who uses the idealized transference with an opposite-gender therapist to denigrate the other spouse, *or* to grow out of the marriage through a kind of "affair" with the therapist. Therapists not cognizant of erotic transferences have only recently realized the folly of over-identification with the in-treatment spouse, and called me in to see the other spouse, or the couple, as a guilt-driven attempt to head off a divorce. These are painful times for all concerned, because during the couple consultation the couple therapist may determine that it is not individual patient growth that is leading to a divorce but the referring therapist's collusion with the patient in degrading the other spouse through a mutually idealizing or erotic enactment. Such are the pressures on the countertransference, with splits and alliances that dominate these special circumstances so that the other spouse may not stand a chance of being understood. When the individual therapy leads to a potential divorce I recommend at least a marital review with therapists specializing in couples. The two partners are seen from the beginning and the task is to decide if terminating the relationship should go forward. Couple therapists value personal and couple growth, so that a fair attempt is made to allow a couple time to mourn the marital loss, or recover a possibility of renewed effort to work together.

Whether therapy is with an individual or a couple, examining transferences and countertransference is a central feature of treatment and is especially important when a frustrated dependency is visited on the unsuspecting therapist.

CONSEQUENCES OF INFIDELITY

Six causes and one consequence of affairs are listed next (Pittman, 1990). Each identifies relational dynamics that underpin the potential for acting out, but the seeds of deception are sown in the couple's tendencies to ignore or deny recent or long-term ruptures in the relationship.

1. If affairs and marriages continue without resolution, conflict will likely escalate; due to affairee demands, such as pressing for a commitment; the offending spouse leaves clues and is found out, or an affair is discovered as a by-product of other reasons to enter therapy that stress the marital container beyond its limit (child-centered case or spousal sexual dysfunction).
2. Spouses may be ignorant as to the changes in their relationship over time but are hitting snags in certain family situations (adolescent sexuality, birth, death, health problems, or other life-stage issues).
3. There may be an increase in spousal narcissistic preoccupations, as in autonomy-dependency fantasies. Sadomasochistic impingements include over-sacrificing, or an increased tendency for self-denigration, or the need to rescue.
4. Perfectionism (idealization); no room for any "bad" objects.

5. Fears of disillusionment; denied emptiness, results in overexcitement, as in the "manic defense." Serial affairs can be one result of flights of manic anxieties.
6. Deficiencies in friendship capacities and loss of commitments.
7. Collusion in the denial of unacceptable qualities in a spouse.

One or more preconditions can contribute to infidelity. We emphasize the unconscious motives behind the conscious decision to stray from monogamy. Next, we present the dynamics of deception, as we find it more devastating to the relationship than sexual infidelity.

THE INTRAPSYCHIC-DEVELOPMENTAL
MEANING OF SECRETS

Due to the importance of deception, and the need for it that accompanies affairs, we want to be aware of the developmental origins of secrets in general, so as to comprehend the underlying meanings of a spouse's more destructive use of secrets within marriage. It is also clinically relevant to recognize that infidelity can be a split-off result of either spouse's incapacity to share secret wishes, worries, or longings, due to their shameful nature, and fears of what the other spouse might do if they knew.

Rather than viewing current marital deceptions as entities in themselves, we use theory that traces and includes a broader spectrum of past developmental contributions as they bear on the inclination to deceive. Often we find that increased use of deception in adult life stems from overuse of defenses in previous dealings with adults as a child, when the child was faced with inordinate confusions about boundaries, and the concurrent anxieties that accompanied issues of mistrust were repressed. In some cases, there are strong tendencies to sadomasochistic/narcissistic pairings in the primary child-caregiver relationship that we see repeated in adult life choices of the marital partner.

The normative childhood basis for secrets stems from a gradually emerging sense of autonomy in separating from the primary parent. Having choices as to what to share about the private mental and physical world of the child is a departure from the almost total dependency of infancy. A child, age five to eight, for example, due to superego development, may deny "wrongdoing" to avoid punishment. It is more than fear, however, that fosters the child's privacy of thought content, and deciding what to share, with whom, and when. Just as the earlier control of bladder and bowel may have been accompanied by pleasurable motives in withholding or adult praise in relinquishing, the older child is learning about separateness and autonomy, as well as social benefits of control over impulses.

Channeling the drives always includes the social choices of who to include in the "telling" and "showing." Is it the trusted pal, family friend, other parent, or sibling? Or will the precious secret be kept only for the self? The developmental process is one of self-interest, socialization, and self-reliance; the ultimate aim of "mastery" is the internalization of impulse and its pleasures and discomforts.

A selective process is now possible with choices of confiding in different objects. Or the "secret" can be kept within the self. Winnicott (1986) makes the important observation that the child needs the freedom to decide, in the "true self" sense, what to communicate only to the self. In healthy development, social conventions are insufficient for motivating disclosures of special self-references or secrets. Privacy implies the capacity to be alone and comfortable with a portion of the self that is not for others' ears or eyes. This process aids in shaping individuality and should not be confused as withdrawal or schizoid retreat, which is anxiety-driven; this milestone should be viewed in developmental terms as a pleasurable private and selectively interactive communication experience.

When this process is blocked by narcissistically intrusive parents and excessive shaming, the child may be forced to keep secrets to maintain self-cohesion in the face of boundary violations. When personal space is endangered, the need to be secretive becomes a malformed defense against ego breakdown due to excessive external demands. The superego becomes primitive and punitive. If the child holds back, then he or she has failed to meet the parents' requirements and may lose their love. If the child submits, the outrage and sense of invasion become dangerous, and the self may feel resentful. The tragic result is that in later life, mistrust (with its overload of shame, fear, and rage over having been robbed of this vital period of development) shapes the marriage through secretiveness. A partner with such a background may never reveal a personal life, and reasonable accountability may be viewed as intrusive and suffocating.

An extramarital affair is but one form of deception. An affair can take on many of the forbidden precursors allowed by the fact of deception, in which sharing the split-off forbidden impulses, dependencies, and desires are accepted. As long as these are kept out of the marriage, where they are assumed to be too dangerous, the unfaithful spouse is able to partially experience the previously blocked affect and attendant gratification, albeit in secret, while avoiding another aim, a more difficult developmental task—intimacy in the marriage.

SYMBOLIC REPRESENTATION OF THE AFFAIREE

The affairee has an important meaning for the couple, well beyond the manifest aspects we are initially presented with. The affairee and the affair are idealized versions of the deep, unconscious ties, attachments, and potentially pathological object relations within each spouse's family tree. This can refer to ties significant adults and peers in a spouse's childhood. As personified in the marriage, the affairee is not a superior choice over the other spouse, difficult as that may be to believe, but rather is a different *object*. The longings, attachments, and gratifications are applied to the affairee. When compared with the marital relationship, the affairee offers the necessary supplies to help manage split-off infantile and adolescent fantasies, without the feared superego constraints centered in the marital negative transference. The therapist studies the fantasy data to explore the denied or avoided issues in the marriage. Also, there may have been several generations of philandering males and females that warded off fears in a manner similar to what the current spouses are doing.

The betrayed spouse may have fantasies about the qualities that the affairee has that would make him or her attractive to the other spouse. Avoidance of under-the-surface marital distress is the major "hotbed" usually giving way to volcanic blame and pain. Affairs shake the couple's values regarding monogamy and intimacy at their deepest levels. It may take time to persuade the couple that the affair represents deeper roots of conflict, such as denied impulses repressed in the marriage, developmental impasses, longstanding unspoken needs, or power imbalances. Pain generally is the powerful emotion that accompanies fear that the marriage is irreparably damaged. Rage may surface. Revenge or compliance may drive the aggrieved spouse, depending on whether they hold themselves responsible or blameless for the affair.

The possibilities accompanying each couple's experience of the throes of the extramarital affair are varied. We therapists are in a vulnerable position in such cases, as the emotions run high and wild and can capture us. We may take sides, get caught up only in damage control functions, or quickly split the couple up in individual sessions if we cannot bear their rage or pain. What we do depends on our personal and clinical experiences and attitudes about deception and unfaithfulness. Our religious or moral feelings can influence our ability to be attentive to their specific relationship history and dynamics and impede our tuning in to their unconscious object relationships.

Awareness of countertransference reactions, therefore, is central to our understanding of these matters. We strive to be open to the manner in which the couple's and our own unconscious valences promote impasse in doing meaningful work. This interplay of couple and therapist projective processes reveals the couple patterns.

COLLUSION AS A DYNAMIC IN TREATMENT

Collusion between spouses in the marriage is a prognostic indicator of outcome in marital treatment. Collusion refers to a combination of delusion (self-deception), illusion (capacity to deceive oneself under a strong wish), and elusion (get away with or play at deception). If there is a strong couple narcissistic preoccupation with blurring objective and subjective parts of self and other, this mutual game of collusion (sometimes related to borderline tendencies), places strain on the therapist's endeavors.

Collusion is a special type of mutual projective identification, because it is a complementary inducement, the willingness to be the embodiment of the split off, denied parts of partner and self. Boundary blurring, histrionic clinging, annihilation fears, and fusion are employed regularly in the pursuit of psychic economy and survival. Each spouse casts off his or her antilibidinal or repressed libidinal strivings. Self-betrayal, self-deception, and self-delusion result. As unconscious forms of communication, however, we can study and comprehend the manner in which grave deprivations occurred in the spouses' past and attempt to address those dynamic forces within the containment process for interpretive or reframing.

A SPECIAL CIRCUMSTANCE WHEN ONE SPOUSE SEEKS TREATMENT WITH A SECRET AFFAIR

This complex case features individual work with a sexually addicted male spouse, who eventually sought help with his marriage, while continuing an affair of some eight months with an associate at work. Eventually, couple work became possible; however, before that occurred, there were extensive strains on the therapist's holding environment.

The case featured an extramarital affair of some eight months, which the male spouse presented initially to the referring social worker at his company employee assistance program (EAP) when looking for help. The affairee was a subordinate of his with whom he worked closely on various projects. An especially interesting aspect of the referral was that the female social worker, who had made referrals to me before and who was an experienced veteran, told me a story of deceit with such anger and mistrust of the patient that when the wife in this case called her for a referral for herself, she had been tempted to break confidence and tell all. Insofar as the social worker had previously been a reliable professional, I was wondering what I was getting myself into, given the pressures on maintaining confidentiality and given the husband's effect on the counselor's countertransference.

The wife had been referred to a female therapist. I usually prefer to see couples together. Given that the wife asked for a referral at the same time as the husband did, I inferred that things had been heating up at home (whether the husband's affair was known or not). The EAP counselor asked me to get back to her about the patient's progress and warned me that he was probably "sociopathic." I told her I would not report on his progress but, in keeping with EAP policy, would let her know if he kept his appointment. I also said that if he wanted to work on the marriage, I would include the other spouse if at all possible. Again, she sympathized with the "unsuspecting" wife.

STRAINS ON HOLDING AND CONTAINING

Marital therapists encountering such cases are in a difficult situation. Our training in object relations couple therapy and personal preferences ordinarily place the clinical emphasis on the marital relationship as the unit of treatment. This type of case may prevent any potential for marital work, even if the spouse in treatment may later seek or go along with a recommendation for marital work. This is due to the "secret" being kept between the spouse and the therapist. The therapist's ambivalence about holding the secret may intensify. If the spouse later decides on marital sessions but clearly wants to keep it that way, the deception sets the stage for a threatened holding environment for both spouses.

Will the one spouse "come clean" to the other spouse, signaling a "renewed" commitment to work on the marriage? Will (s)he leave the marriage for the significant other, who possesses "none" of the "irritants" or "aggravations" centered in the marriage? Superimposed on these issues is the therapist's level of comfort. Are we colluding to keep the "affair" going with our patient? Do we identify strongly with the (as yet unseen) spouse and wish to protect him or her, or do we advocate sharing the secret, perhaps prematurely, so we can get "off the hook" with our moral dilemma (assuming we have some positive feelings about monogamy)? Central to our therapeutic position is the issue of whom and what we treat.

The stage is now set to delve into the clinical experience, which will address what to do in such situations. One bias should be noted: The psychoanalytic object relations approach assumes that unconscious motives are often conflicted due to previous traumas, failures in trust, and skewed attempts at paired relationships. We hope to comprehend the intrapsychic dimensions of the patient's circumstances. We want to employ the concept of the *internal couple* during the early stages of assessment. This concept refers to the patient's internalized pairing experiences since childhood, including each child-parent dyadic features of the parents' marital relationship, and sibling pairings. Internalized object relations are based on all significant pairings. In addition to family relations, we also trace pairings attempted from adolescence through young adulthood. Conscious and unconscious choices of the marital partner are viewed in light of what was accomplished or experienced as failures in previous bonding and the ways the new choice may attempt to repair or repeat narcissistic wounds.

The discovery process takes time. If possible, and if the patient can be amenable to this task of discovery, we may be best served to wait and work with what comes from sessions to determine what limit setting or recommendations to make about the patient's deceit (and its negative impact) if there is to be any therapeutic progress. We consider how the patient is using us to hold the secret(s), while promoting a need to have the marriage continue on some basis and continuing the affair. Splitting of this type is not surprising in many clinical situations, so we attempt to work with it in terms of the transference in the here and now and as an important aspect of the patient's core ambivalence. It is helpful to point out a mixture of conflicting motives without being judgmental. Conflicting motives can be situational or characterological, so it is prudent to observe the flow of content and the narratives about them before determining our approach. I am emphasizing that our containment and patient monitoring of the clinical process distinguishes in-depth work from authoritarian or "quick-fix motivational" approaches.

Should the intake spouse prefer individual therapy, however, the issue of holding, or challenging the secret, can shift temporarily or completely from the marriage as the unit of treatment. Instead, issues of betrayal, ambivalence, deception, avoidance, and their possible oedipal derivatives may become the focus in the individual therapy. There may be many other secrets being held by the patient, some not in awareness. We are not obliged to force the patient into a premature decision because we feel ambivalent or torn in our role as a marital therapist. We are now working with an individual, while thinking about the couple and the affairee, with whom we may identify because we, like him or her, are also holding a secret from the other spouse. The pressure on the holding and containment functions of the therapist is great.

CASE MATERIAL ILLUSTRATING MOVEMENT FROM INDIVIDUAL TO COUPLE TREATMENT

Harold presented as a well-groomed, good-looking, and fit young man, thirty-three-years old, articulate, agitated, and making little eye contact at first. He had an anxious smile as he related his story: a ten-year marriage to Sandra, two young children (a three-year-old son and six-year-old daughter), a good job with a future, and a life in many ways improved over his previous circumstances. He had left many positions in his work life, some business partnerships, some entrepreneurial. He never stuck with anything for too long, because he tended to paint himself into corners; either by not working hard enough or by deceiving others into believing he could deliver when he could not. He spoke deliberately and fluently, asking nothing of me except to listen, talking of himself as a chameleon. He focused on the work history as a way of communicating his current situation, I thought, and perhaps his entire lot in life. He had gone into debt, paid a lot back, and now had good opportunities but was anxious about whether he had what it took to succeed.

I asked why he had requested the referral for therapy. He mentioned that the affair was something he had fallen into (reminding me of the Lifeline TV commercial where an elderly person says,

"I've fallen and I can't get up" and presses the help button); it just happened. He admitted that he was in love with Barbara (26) but did not know about giving up his marriage. He was confused and felt he could continue to have his own way because he could always get his way with Sandra, whether it was going out to meetings or playing sports (or having an affair). The affair had been going on for eight months, and he was worried that Barbara would leave her husband and that he would be tempted to be with her. I asked him to compare his wife with the girlfriend and discovered that the major difference he initially saw was that Barbara made him feel he was special, in love-making in particular. I asked for elaboration. Sandra was in Overeaters Anonymous (OA); she had gained weight in the marriage, and he was turned off by that. Though his wife had lost weight in recent years and was fit now, he saw in Barbara an exciting, all-approving, vulnerable woman, unhappily married, with an extraordinary ability to make him feel so good that he in return felt a completeness that he could not experience in his marriage. He also described Sandra as an independent, self-sufficient woman. When he spoke of his children a little later, he saddened. He did not want to hurt them. He also realized how foolish he was to be seeing someone at his company but remarked how he had been able to talk his way out of every kind of confrontation since grade school (I wondered if he was expecting this of me and putting me on notice he was prepared to talk his way out of anything I had to say that might challenge him).

I offered him time to spend together to explore the deeper motives in his life and his basis for wanting help. Because he had been getting away with his secret for so long, why now? I raised both issues, the dilemmas such as being closer to success, not wanting to hurt the children, wanting to be complete and secure, and the need for a woman he could please and receive a special feeling from. The marriage seemed to be lacking in some areas, but he wasn't certain that leaving it was the next step. I also asked, if he left the marriage and married Barbara, would there be any ebbing in the glow of the emotional and sexual excitement? He agreed to come and explore.

Salient Dynamics in the Short-Term Individual Therapy

In the three months of weekly sessions that followed, we explored his early life to current situation. A physically abusive mother died when he was sixteen, after a four-year painful cancer. He never mourned her. Father was described as an obsessive and distant figure, who saw life as something to be endured (except for tennis, which he loved). Sister, three years older than Harold, and he had an incestuous relationship when he was twelve and she was fifteen. Harold recalled being forced to scrub the bathroom floor once per week, while father went to play tennis. Few feelings were expressed during the reciting of these circumstances. As the story of his life unfolded, a crippling sensation entered the countertransference: rage, fear, erotic overstimulation, retaliation, etc., not conscious in Harold, emerged as intellectual awareness in me. I, uncharacteristically, did not feel compassion for him. Rather, I was flooded by dread. I was containing the affects repressed by him on the one hand and was feeling attacked by his unconscious "hateful mother" and abused "self" (subject and object sets). I was at first unclear concerning my own defenses against feeling, while "hating" Harold for subjecting me to his schizoid retreat from all pain. As I looked further, I wondered if I was also holding his family's displaced/projected "rage" and acting it out by my lack of compassion, perhaps in identification with the "lovelessness" in the family. As I listened to him, my intellect was active and alive (as was his), but my emotions were relegated to a deeper place of safety (as were his).

His sexual proclivities began at age fifteen (I considered the coincidence given sister's age at incest) when he also spent most of his time out of the home to avoid mother's intimidation, demandingness, and abuse. He ran away to Florida that year, called home wishing they would miss him, but they asked if he was all right, sent money, and blamed him for causing trouble.

In the course of this exploration, he became coincidentally interested in his marital relationship. I had not prodded him or directed the conversation at this early stage, but listened actively, processing within myself the implications of his history. I concluded that he had unconsciously, due to the holding in the setting, worked up the curiosity to ask, for the first time, had he really worked on the marriage? Though the affair was still important to him, the first appearance of ambivalence, in the form of a mild self-confrontation, emerged. I was aware of feeling emotionally separate from him. I wondered if his story about his acting out had stirred some punitive or benevolent guilt in me about his treatment of his wife; I was feeling like parents who did not miss him when he ran away, which would have confirmed his feelings of despair and rage at being unloved. He also internalized their accusation/belief that he was a troublemaker.

He was a troublemaker. He was making trouble for me because I had to continue to remain neutral. Acting out his appetites disturbed me. I did not like him. To my knowledge, no reconciliation had occurred between him and his mother, father, or sister; there were no conversations about the past. Was he capable of remorse, given his "justification" for seeking gratification/soothing through extramarital sex, sports, alcohol, and the obsession with feeling special, by saving his affairee (his father's hobbies came to mind—the escape from feeling)? I was feeling aspects of his splitting—the unmet love and the hate experiences that left him at an infantile level of attachment. My compassionate side was split off, due to an identification (a preoccupation) with his spouse, who would hate and distrust him if she knew of the affair. I wondered if his ambivalence would grow. Could he tolerate this disturbance enough to explore it further? Or would he re-repress it due to the pain inherent in allowing these hidden feelings to surface?

Another important process was running parallel to his early sessions. His wife was in therapy too and was recently asking him about Barbara. (I learned later on in the conjoint therapy that Sandra's therapist had been supervised by me some years before, so perhaps her orientation as a marital therapist was finding its way into Sandra's "ready" psyche). With these pressures now coming from Sandra, I offered to see the couple so that Harold could examine his split between the two women by examining the marriage in particular. He was recognizing that the time for pretending was passing. His life consisted of one deception after another, and he realized that his house of cards would soon fall. At first, he could not consider telling Sandra about the affair; he wanted marital sessions and individual therapy to continue. I went along with him on a temporary basis, with a focus on his deep fears of facing the possibility that Sandra might throw him out; he chuckled like a small boy, wanting to be caught and fearing being caught. He had been deceiving her for a long time; how could he respect himself if things continued? To my surprise he said that he would reduce and eventually terminate the affair with Barbara. My internal experience of this was to have my doubts that he could give up anything that kept him gratified, given his addictive nature.

I was willing to see the couple to determine how the spousal relationship was set up to maintain collusion and splitting of libidinal and aggressive impulses and also to assess the strengths of the relationship. Turmoil, unconscious desires, past object relations, and the meaning of children interested me as we began. I was also a bit relieved that I might not have to hold the "secret" much longer, hoping that if couple work was not possible, each spouse would still be able to continue individual therapy toward some shift in the status quo. Indeed the status quo had already shifted due to Sandra's individual treatment.

Sandra and Harold Begin Couple Therapy

Early couple sessions revealed that Sandra (a tall brunette) was an intelligent match for Harold and was two inches taller than he. Her background consisted of two alcoholic parents and two sisters, she the youngest. She remembered being left alone a lot, not being listened to, and being attracted to and fearful of her father, because he physically intimidated her. He played the wrist-rope game with her as a youngster, in which he would encircle her wrist with his hand and make friction until her wrist burned. He would then laugh. He also sometimes did that to her two children. She also reported having been touched on her breast by a male gym teacher at age fourteen, a vague recollection of date rape at age eighteen (she had been drinking), and blurred memories of possible molestation by her father during early childhood. She cried at the sharing of these tragic memories (in contrast to Harold's stoicism). He sat and stared ahead as she spoke, as though waiting for Sandra to attack him for being "another" abusive male. She did not attack him in the initial sessions. At first, she tested Harold by a combination of "little girl" gentle inquiries about Barbara. In later sessions, tearful and depressed, Sandra became furious and physically threatening (at home, she hit walls with her feet and threw objects at him).

In other sessions, I learned of Harold's many affairs. She seemed at the bursting point at times, and I wondered if any work at comprehending and containing was possible. Would she throw him out, would he leave due to the intolerable violence against him, stay together because of the children, or would the violence escalate until someone was physically injured? Harold had not told her the truth. I indicated in individual sessions that her panic over not knowing was leading to physical violence.

As individual sessions continue, I suggest she wants to know if he intends to stay or go. Does he love Barbara enough? I share that Sandra's being out of control is due to being held hostage to Harold's nondisclosure. He is fearful of losing Barbara *and* Sandra. He becomes more anxious and depressed. He admits to being an active drinker. He wants to tell the truth even though he may not be able to get over the loss of Barbara. He wants to work on the marriage. He admits to having used cocaine until his son was born, and he wants to use it again. He rehearses the moment of painful confession. It arrives in the fifth couple session.

A SESSION ILLUSTRATING THE CONFESSION

Admission of the Affair

Harold confesses his affair with Barbara the morning before the couple's fifth session.

Background to Session 5

In the fourth session, Sandra pressed Harold to explain why he had been so remote. Harold's responses were less than candid, and I continued to hold his secret, bearing considerable guilt over knowing the truth that Sandra was seeking. Since the couple had begun marital therapy, I felt a countertransference of collusion with Harold, as though I was the affairee, continuing my betrayal of Sandra. I retained my position, in spite of the personal discomfort in the hope that the individual work with Harold would bring out the deception, and I might work on the split with the couple. I worried that Sandra would hold me responsible for keeping the secret and break off the therapy, even if Harold came clean, and she might not understand why I chose to be patient with the process.

The day before Harold confessed the affair, Sandra telephoned me expressing desperation over Harold's increased aloofness, sulking, and unresponsiveness. She felt terrified about what Harold was keeping from her, so she could not wait until the next session, and pressed me for advice on how to handle her panic. In asking her what she imagined Harold's behavior could be about, she blurted out her worst fears—that he was having an affair, wanted to leave her and the children, and was afraid to tell her.

In Harold's most recent individual session, he spoke of depression and of building the courage to tell Sandra of the eight-month-long affair. Then, I received Harold's cell phone call the day of their couple session announcing with great anxiety that he had spilled it and that they were on their way to my office. I expected the fallout to come through the door. I felt considerable relief that the secret could finally be discussed, but this was accompanied by a worry at the potential for violence, principally associated with Sandra's explosive temper.

"T." refers to the therapist.
"H." refers to the husband.
"W." refers to the wife.

Session 5

They entered the office, actually bolted through the door and sat down in their usual places. They stared at me.

T.: So, what was said this morning, who said it and where did things go from there? (Customarily I do not begin sessions, but my anxiety forced this departure to get to the fallout as quickly as possible.)

(Silence)

T.: (I was not able to bear the silence more than fifteen seconds.) By the way, this has been long overdue.

H.: It doesn't matter, well it does. We were. . . .

W.: He knows we spoke by phone—and I asked him. . . .

H.: She's been, I've been in a bad state this week. She asked, "Are you planning on leaving? Can we talk about it?" It's not the easiest thing to talk about (looking at me). I had to think on it on my own; put it off on the side. She kept, "What is it, I don't understand—something you're not telling me." Something from inside me said let's get the truth out.

W.: He didn't say it that way.

H.: No, I didn't say it that way. I grabbed her arms within a few seconds of saying it—I knew she was going to swing at me. I told her I had an affair with B. First she cried.

W.: No, it's not what I did first.

H.: She said she felt bad for me.

W.: I said it must have been hard for you.

H.: Then, she's beginning to understand why I've been the way I've been for awhile. And then she got angry.

W.: I walked out of the room, the overwhelming anger was unbelievable.

H.: Punching me and kicking the walls.

W.: (Screaming while at home) I hate you, I hate you.

H.: The kids were home.

W.: Sabrina (6) came running, "Who are you yelling I hate you to?"

I'm very angry at your father and I'm yelling at him, but you can go back in and watch TV. I'm sorry I'm being too loud. (Turning to me) What was I going to do?

(I silently observed that each spouse is speaking the words they spoke that morning as if they are still there and not here.)

T.: How much is on the table? (They've been subdued thus far, except that when S. quotes herself, her voice raises.)

W.: I don't know Carl, I don't know (she's getting angry). I want to know everything. Is it his first affair? Is it the only affair? How long it's been going on, how many times he fucking, fucked her? He says he doesn't know. Oh, that many goddamn many fucking times?

(She pauses, becomes tearful . . . depressed.)

I hate him so much! He broke my glasses in the car. (Crying openly.)

H.: What I hear in the car (He is restrained, looking down, in a whisper) is, "I don't trust you, obviously." (Now he looks up, tense, tight lipped, seething, I surmise, but still very subdued.) "I don't believe a word you say to me."

W.: You've told me I can't trust you and I can't believe anything you say.

H.: You said to me, "I don't believe you, I don't want you talking to anyone I care about, and you're a horrible father, and I don't want you near the kids."

W.: I didn't say that—where were you when you did it? Were you supposed to be reading stories to your children, when you were supposed to be working?

H.: (Quoting S.) How can you pretend to even love your kids?

W.: (Bristling) I said that because if you can be so irresponsible as this—and I don't know if you wore condoms, he told me he did, and I could be infected with a fucking virus, it scares me. Excuse me (looking at me and lowering her eyes). I can't believe him. Can he finally be saying something I can believe? He swore up and down to me he didn't have an affair with this whore; I know where she works. I don't care what happens to him at work. And at this moment (really worked up, angry, desperate) I am going after her. I've got people behind me. My family will financially support me. And then . . . I'm sitting in the car and I want to hold his hand and I want to hug and kiss him, because I love him, and I'm so mad at him. I'm not mad that he had the affair and that he's been lying to me about it. I'm past the affair. Because I thought he had it a long time ago.

T.: You did?

W.: I told everybody, I think he's having an affair. Trust your instincts, Sandra. . . . Well I've asked him again and again. He's not totally responsible for this—she spread her legs for him. God knows how many times, where, and when. She not only screwed her boss, she screwed her boss, she screwed another man's, another woman's husband, who has children; and I can't believe there's a God in heaven who shines down on her, and says that she too shall be healed. I don't care what pain she was in, but I care about him, and I hate the fact he's going through pain . . . but now he's just as mad as I am.

T.: Harold, why did you decide to tell Sandra about it? Being that you decided to tell her, did you have a goal in mind? Where do you want this to lead? What led you to Barbara is still there, and Sandra's instincts were correct. Both of you are having to face the fallout, and the basis for the affair.

(I feel that Sandra's intensely painful, and confused state requires a response from H. that might bring out his motives for the admission.)

W.: This morning he said he still thinks about wanting to be with her and what does that mean? I need clarification from him.

T.: Yes, I see. Problems in trust and reliability are there, but they predate the affair. That is not to minimize the betrayal and its meaning to both of you, but I want to open up discussion about your marriage. Harold, say more about why you want Sandra to know.

H.: The truth is I am selfish, and I burden myself. She might throw me out and save me the trouble of working on the problems. I am a very mixed up person. I get confused about where I belong so I thought S. would decide what we should do—I'd have no choice; the decision to stay or go could come from S., her deciding for me. It sounds stupid, but if I left my marriage the reason would be clear. Not complicated—I had an affair; my wife threw me out.

T.: Simple, but not the sum of its parts; consistent, though, with your history. You get into big trouble, flee, or get the other to punish you.

H.: I'm not sure I want to go on with my marriage, and I don't understand how S. would want us to go on together.

T.: You look to S. to take away your confusion; learning about your motives in the marriage, past and present, means having to stay with very unpleasant feelings. Telling her the truth this morning is the tip of the iceberg, but I imagine it took some courage.

T.: (This is my opportunity to address both of them.) I think the affair and its painful surfacing has importance in many ways. To you (Sandra) it feels like a disaster, yet you want to hold on to Harold. For you (Harold) it could be a way out of ambivalence, but maybe before you face some complex issues. On the other hand, by being here you each have a chance to learn about hidden areas of the relationship, shaky in many respects, but not addressed before.

W.: I'm confused, but I want him; I don't know why right now (tearful).

H.: I'm afraid to go home with her; the violence makes me want to run.

T.: Sandra's need for you may make you fearful too, because you are torn between two women, and you can't guarantee you'll stay.

They discuss how to manage at home until the next session. Each agrees that they will try to keep it together for the children. We schedule an additional session that week. End of session.

Shared Spousal Dynamics

Spousal dynamics in common included family-of-origin traumatogenic factors, including incest and physical abuse, alcoholism, with damaging boundary diffusion, and inconsistencies of over and under involvement of a primarily narcissistic nature between parents and children. Each spouse displayed fragmentation of internal capacities to bear frustration and pain, with regressive pulls to addictive substances, and omnipotent fantasies of having control. There was a shared desperate dependency on the marriage, with the resultant disillusionment, schizoid retreat, and use of each other as temporary gratifiers. The pathological marital fit I was working with was borderline-schizoid and the couple's core projective dynamics were sadomasochistic (McCormack, 2000). Sadomasochism was evidenced by maternal and paternal failures and manipulations suffered in childhood. The spouses' sets of parents distorted dependency needs, and intimidated and suppressed feelings and perceptions in their children because they conflicted with their narcissistic motives. The tragic result was that the spouses maintained a borderline-masochistic relationship and a growing precarious hold on internal and external reality.

The paranoid-schizoid position predominates and narrows the capacity for thinking, responding, and remembering. When confronted with the affairs, the basic ego structures (so predominated by suspicion, insecurity, desperate attachment, and self-doubt) splinter further, threatening not only the marriage but also each spouse's ability to function. Splitting, which characterizes the defense against depressive anxieties, was most apparent in Harold. His ongoing bouts with drinking further impeded getting closer to the repressed depressive and abandonment feelings and fears. A common catastrophe I noted in their respective childhoods was incest; Harold by an older sister, Sandra by her father. Common traumas caused blurring between the generations and in the marriage they shared negative expectations that any relationship could be reliable or stable.

Sandra represented his attempt to bond with a maternal figure, but she lacked the excitement required to ward off Harold's unconscious terror at being either abandoned or dominated. Sandra was recently becoming more independent, eliciting unconscious fears of his not being special. Barbara represented the needed excitement in the sexual realm, and she needed to be saved, which was even more exciting, enhancing Harold's rescue fantasy and wish for Oedipal triumph. There would be no room for depressing feelings, loss, or forgiveness. These repressed issues were at the core of Harold's internal object relations pathology.

His extramarital acting out was spurred by ambivalence about whether to stay married to Sandra, because having another woman could allow him to remain between the two, but not with either fully, causing a temporary delay in making any decision. And the constant deception added to his distress. The weakening of his defenses, and a growing panic that any decision could resolve his longings for nirvana, led to the confession and was the catalyst for moving the couple into exploring the considerable pain of fragmentation in the marital ego.

One consequence of the rupture in the already-shaky marital trust was a short-term psychiatric hospitalization. Harold became suicidal soon after his confession. The strain of confronting the reality of giving up Barbara, and having to focus on the loss of her as the idealized love object, unleashed unbearable shame and guilt, and a depression so painful that he called me during an alcohol-induced panic threatening to crash his car. During his hospital stay, we continued marital sessions onsite with the cooperation of the attending psychiatrist. Upon discharge, they continued intensive marital work for two years.

Results of Intensive Marital Work

In-depth marital treatment reworked couple and individual deficits and restored couple safety in the marital bond. Sandra continued in OA and Harold began attending Alcoholics Anonymous. The twelve-step supportive groups significantly helped to stabilize the spouses and supplemented the therapy. The suicidal crisis resulted in both spouses getting in touch with early childhood pain and terror. They were able to mentalize the core terrors in the safety of the treatment and that established containment in the marriage; previously their unmetabolized pain had led to rage and splitting. The depressive features, denied by both spouses in the course of their lives were also revealed. The couple recognized the annihilative threats originated in prior family life, and each came to understand and modify rages at the abuse each had suffered in the past. By tracing the deficits to childhood, they re-owned the mutual projections and lifted some of the burden from their marriage. Moderate restoration of mutual and self-regulation occurred, with the working through of infantile dependencies. Better couple holding resulted, improving their capacity to nurture the relationship and accept life's limitations.

Surface-to-depth treatment was illustrated in this complex case of short-term individual therapy combined with long-term couple treatment. I assessed the presenting problems and reframed them for eventual in-depth treatment. I viewed the husband's persistent need for an affair while holding on to his conflicted marriage as the initial problem. I sensed there were deep layers that might be accessible if we moved slowly through his initial concerns. From the outset, my aim was not to panic or to be unduly pressed to "change" him to resolve my ambivalence and moral disturbance about the duplicity. It would have been easy to become impatient, so I kept in mind that I had an individual who was in pain, whose behavior had luckily forced him into treatment. I learned that his troubled marriage was an important relationship, even though there was an ongoing affair. I first thought from the psychological surface of his problem (stay with the affair and leave the marriage, or give it up and be miserable in the marriage). We worked with a theme that his search for bliss in intimacy had gone wrong. It became clear that a centered holding would be essential/fundamental if there was to be any movement through his internal split. This had to become important to establish a rationale for marital therapy.

He was able to accept marital work because he realized the ambiva-lence he carried was multiply motivated; that the marriage was not the only contributing factor to his problems with life.

The depth of his narcissistic injuries, grandiosity, and entitle-ment stemmed from lifelong struggles with autonomy-dependency issues. His wife suffered from a sadomasochistic object constella-tion. The two partners joined malignant disorders that ran deep, and they surfaced slowly for enough movement for eventual marital reparation and a new beginning. We keep in mind that unconscious motives for mate selection play an important part in the shaping of needs and frustrations due to the inevitable emerging of bad object relations. These deep-seated personality and relational issues were best worked with by attending to the husband's current behaviors in the context of good-enough holding and as stemming from unpro-cessed historical deficits and traumatic neglect. Once minimal trust in me was established, the marital relationship, as the reader will note, could then receive needed attention, and the wife's back-ground and personality issues further informed me of the husband and wife's disturbed marital fit. The steps taken in this case are rather unusual as the mixture of individual and couple therapies with the same therapist is atypical. As stated earlier in the book, couple therapists are capable of multi-contextual thinking about the individual and the couple so that both vertices inform the choices of modalities.

Chapter Seven

Accessing the Internal World of Couples through Their Dreams

A SHORT ESSAY ON DREAMS AND DEVELOPMENT TO SET THE STAGE

Dreams are the unconscious poetry and prose of the internal object world. They are art and truth that take form as hidden mysteries, echoing individual and relational narratives, whose understanding is vital to an integration of past life with future possibilities. Our vulnerability to unconscious limitations stems from limited insight. Consciousness about life is overestimated as sufficient for adequate functioning and ambition, much in the way a materialistic world is preferred over an ambiguous and shadowy inner world. In the dark world that lies beneath our trappings, available during sleep, our vulnerabilities are at their peak. There is great potential to melt the darkness and to illuminate the precious and precarious parts of the self and object world. If ready, the multitude of unacknowledged concerns, longings, dreads, and search strategies emerge, at first in the form of vague awarenesses, or in scary nightmares, from which we are so glad to awaken. We pinch ourselves in reassurance: "It was *only* a dream." If these echoes, presented to us at first as vague and inchoate, are grounded in a proper language and environment for exploration, the sounds and images can be decoded for deep personal understanding.

But not so fast! Do we really want to know what lies within? There are the nightmares, so sudden in shock and disturbance at the beginning of childhood, reflecting the developmental push, or impulse to consciousness of not-quite-repressed aggressive, sexual, and familial tumults. Re-repression is the customary outcome unless the child is forced to share the sources of the nighttime distress. As the child cries out, partly asleep, but dimly awake in the night's terror, the parents, who are partly the sources of the disturbance, are called upon to comfort and soothe so as to ameliorate the internal calamity without tampering with it. The child's emotionally charged secrets are returned to the innocence of sleep. Not so in the analytic process, the aim of which is self-consciousness. No sleeping allowed in analysis.

Objectives

I illustrate two dimensions of in-depth couple therapy process that dream work enhances: The first dimension is the elaboration of the unconscious matrix of the couple relationship, and the second concerns transference material that informs the therapist on how therapy is going. In dream work, there are the dream space, room space, and life-space. The *dream space* is the intrapsychic container, which can have the properties of symbolizing unconscious process and deadening psychic process by concrete operations. The *room space* is the therapist as a receptive object, with the couple providing reverie for the potential mentalizing of the dream from the unbearable to the symbolic. The *life-space* refers to here-and-now and there-and-then references in the dream identifying the developmental catastrophe and search strategy for going on being in the individual and the couple. Dreams also illuminate individual and couple transferences by identifying couple developmental issues and conflicts stirred up in the therapeutic triangle. Couple dreams deepen the treatment. Vignettes illustrate the ways each spouse uses free association in working with dreams. Transference-countertransference valences will also be discussed.

THE CLINICAL USEFULNESS OF COUPLE DREAMS

Dreams provide a richness of unconscious relational material in an accessible form. Freud (1900) made the time honored point, "The interpretation of dreams is the royal road to a knowledge of the unconscious activities of the mind" (p. 608). Applied to couples, I would augment the above with "Dreams are the couple's intersection of collective affective unconscious process."

Dream material amplifies the couple's interpsychic narratives, particularly as revelations of therapeutic process, through shadow, mystery, and complexity. Individual spouses often have dreams during the course of treatment, and, on occasion, both spouses will have dreams that overlap or amplify individual and couple issues. Dreams produce images and affects in couples in contrast with the concrete presentations in sessions. Dream material affects the senses of all participants, including the therapist. Dreams bring forth aspects of individual and couple cultures. In marriage, each partner's unconscious intergenerational inheritance shapes attitudes, beliefs, and moral proscriptions. A couple that fails in producing shared meanings relies on fixed beliefs as modes for relating. Each partner's culture must be revisited and renegotiated with concessions made for the sake of a new system. Dreams open up and alert the couple and the therapist to personal identifications and loyalties to ancestors disguised as ghosts that preempt intimate couple relating. Most couples have not considered their own individual histories as factors (objects) that prevent mutuality and satisfaction in the marital relationship. Instead, accusations and criticisms abound as to the other partner's shortcomings with little awareness of what is being carried in the self that drives the differences. This phenomenon of splitting characterizes mildly to severely regressed couples.

We explore the ways dreams represent the internal object worlds of self and family, past and present. Shared unconscious objects abound in the marital relationship in the form of projective identifications. The labyrinth of couple unconscious object relations is available through each spouse's dreams, and analytic work can go deep when experienced in a sitting-up narration of what spouses cannot easily decipher when lying down. What one spouse dreams usually involves the partner, the marriage, and other significant pairings. As we shall see, dreams would include the therapist-spousal triangle. Analysis of couple dreams has a multidimensional value: the dreams of one spouse can illuminate the projective matrix of both. Each spouse may dream on the same occasion, adding breadth to the overall meanings in the marriage relationship. Lastly, couple dreams may ameliorate resistances due to the tamper-proof nature of a dream.

The couple's interpsychic continuum seeks expression. Split-off aspects of introjected object relations live as the subtext of dreams for each spouse. Linkages can be made between the intrapsychic and interpsychic meanings of couple projections. The depth and breadth of these internal communications may represent underlying psychic conflict; elaboration of repressed affects; a shift from one developmental level to another; dramatization to master anxiety and control flooding, longings, hurts or failures in development; transferences to the therapist or spouse; and re-finding lost objects. The reporting of dreams in the company of one's spouse brings to the couple system projective identifications that can become known through the dreamer's interpretations, spouse's responses, and therapist's further analysis of the couple intrapsychic-interpersonal narrative. Dreams freeze the action, making possible a more dispassionate inquiry that uncovers the power of the unconscious. Because the dream is the property of the dreamer and imagination is hard to refute, playing with dream material becomes contagious. They are neither true nor false; hence there is a freedom for the couple to make *mental mudpies*, as the threat of a persecutory superego is reduced.

FOLLOWING THE AFFECT
IN DREAM INTERPRETATION

Midge (28) and Tom (31) had been living together for two years and had been trying to work through in couple therapy their aversion to getting married. Four months into the treatment, Tom reported a dream in which he was driving with Midge to my office. He said that they had driven up and down steep hills, with sharp turns, and he really had to push the car to make it up the hills. Coming down was much easier. Near the end of the journey, coming down the last hill, the car began to speed up, and Tom found that he couldn't break fast enough. He said that as he and Midge neared my office, a stone wall suddenly appeared, and he had to crash into it to stop the car. The car was damaged, but they were okay. I came out to help them out of the car. Once out of the car, Tom saw that there were cliffs below. He concluded that if he and Midge had not hit the stone wall, they would have plunged into the ocean.

I first approach dreams through the dreamer's associations, then the spouse's associations; if I have something to add, I speak last. When I am mentioned in dreams as a particular figure in the life of the spouse or couple, I examine my countertransference to their portrayal of me, so as to locate what type of object I represent—an ego ideal, deprecated part of the self, frightening intrusion, an exciting or elusive object, Oedipal parent, or buddy. Tom said that the dream had disturbed him; he awoke perspiring. He woke Midge up, and they cuddled, but they did not discuss what he had experienced.

He chose to wait until the session. This was typical of Midge and Tom, who tended to veer away from areas of worry in favor of the physical comfort they received from each other and valued highly. In the session, however, Tom was eager to continue. He elaborated on his responsibility as the driver. Midge was in his car, and he was endangering her life. It occurred to him that the frightening ups and downs of the steep hills represented marriage, and the outside world represented challenge and danger. The car was the real culprit, however, because he could not push it hard enough up the hill or stop it on the final descent.

Hearing his associations, Midge could not contain herself with excitement. She thought that the dream dramatized Tom's fear of inadequacy. She said that it not only held him back in his work life, where he was overqualified for the job he did; it also interfered with his getting married. Tom responded by saying that he wasn't sure if he could remain committed to marriage, because his parents had divorced and two of his three brothers were in disastrous marriages.

I said that Tom was in touch with the meaning of the part of the dream where the car went out of control: it signified to him the return of his terror that he would destroy them both if he married and impregnated Midge. Referring to a recent session in which Tom had chuckled playfully about having children with Midge and being a good father, I added that the part of the dream where the downhill road seemed manageable could represent his openness to marriage, after a period of strain and toil in therapy. Tom remembered that in that session Midge had expressed reservations about how she could deal with motherhood, given her background of neglect and deprivation. This comment helped me see that Tom and Midge had a shared view that marriage would lead to disaster, yet they had demonstrated a shared willingness to face their fears. The symbolic meaning of the stone wall brought a mutual acknowledgment. They responded by pointing to the stone wall in the dream:

They concluded that therapy might have been a good barrier against disaster, but at the same time their fears and doubts had been stonewalling the therapy, in case analytic exploration would lead to greater imagined danger.

It was time to examine my countertransference to the dream. I felt like the man who could not prevent the couple from crashing the car. Nor could I remove neither the threat of the ocean nor their ultimate fear: death. I told them that the issue of feared dependency was embedded in the dream, speaking to them in the session, and they saw me as one to help them, but almost too late. They were questioning the holding and containing function of the therapist. Tom made the point that remaining single, but cohabiting with Midge ensured independence for them.

In my countertransference to the dream, I felt I could not prevent the couple from crashing the car. Nor could I remove the threat of the ocean or their ultimate terror: death. True, I helped them out of the car, but I had not been able to save them from going on that harrowing journey. They did still make it to the session but at great risk. At that moment, I questioned my adequacy and holding function. Then I realized they were doing better than I was with analyzing the dream. For Tom and Midge, the dream had activated the encapsulated unconscious; far from depressing them, it was enlivening them and their capacity to work together. At first, I failed to recognize this accomplishment, because I became overly concerned about analyzing the symbolic meaning of the dream and neglected to fully take in the cathartic experience of the dreamer in telling the dream, or the alleviation of anxiety that the couple felt because of working with it. No matter how well aspects may be dissected and analyzed, the full therapeutic potential of the dream cannot be realized until we appreciate the affect of the dreamer and the other spouse during the telling of the dream.

I now saw that the dream was enabling Tom and Midge to confront and master their desperate need for safety and their fears of breakdown and catastrophe. Their fear of depending on each other and on me was embedded in the dream. I said that they saw me as one to help them, but they were afraid that it was almost too late and so might lead to the death of the couple. Tom said that he now realized that he had been living with the fantasy that remaining single, even though cohabitating could ensure independence and therefore a measure of safety for each of them. Working on the dream took Tom and Midge over the wall of their resistances to further work on securing their commitment to remaining a couple.

DISCOVERING THE INTERPERSONAL MEANING OF A DREAM

Linda (48) was making succotash (lima beans and corn). A friend walked in, and she said to her friend that she must be surprised at what Linda was making. Linda felt tense in the dream.

Linda gave me her first association to the dream. She said that she liked corn, and her husband liked lima beans (Scharff and Bagnini, 2001).

Both vegetables retain their individual forms even after prolonged cooking. The word *succotash* makes it sound as if the beans and corn have softened and become mush. Like the beans and corn, Linda and her husband, Rob (50), retained their own individual forms, unmodified by the marriage.

Linda went on the say that she and Rob were incompatible in many ways. It seemed to her that her dream referred to her conflict over the marriage and to her guilt about her wishes to leave Rob. She was further reminded of the powerful guilty feelings she had experienced after her grandmother's death, when she developed a longstanding phobia. She feared that if she left Rob, the guilt would cause the phobia to return. Rob responded that he did not want to be with her if he was just there to prevent a phobia. They went on to talk about the fierce competitiveness between them over the years, which prevented intimate connecting.

I suggested the failure to combine their two personalities like two vegetables for a new flavor in the marriage was the couple's major disappointment. The retaining of separate selves versus achieving a reliable dependency signaled anger. They agreed sadly and went on to voice regret about the wasted years.

For couples in trouble, excessive independence may hide deep-seated fears over being controlled. Fears of domination are dynamics presented and repeated in the therapy. Dreams bypass resistances to understanding as they bring out the intrapsychic bases for the distrust. They surface when there is a proper holding environment and when the unknown qualities of inner experiences are sought. When we solicit dreams, the spouses cross the border from the privacy of the individual unconscious to the interpersonal realm not previously available in the spousal relationship.

DREAM REVEALING HIDDEN AFFECTS OF A NARCISSISTIC-MASOCHISTIC PROJECTIVE MARITAL MATRIX

Background

Seth (60) and Julie (54) were in couple treatment for three months with me, and Seth was in individual sessions with me which began four months ago; Julie was in ongoing psychoanalysis with a colleague (the referral source) prior to the couple work. Seth presented as essentially schizoid (flat affect and overly contained) and began sessions with a concern over what to do as the family business was sold because it was losing money, and he, as CFO, did not want to go to work for the European company that was buying them out. The CEO was his brother-in-law (wife's brother), and they had never gotten along in thirty years, and they hardly communicated unless absolutely necessary. Seth referenced Julie in most of the early sessions, pointing out that she wanted to continue working after he retired. This fact seemed to make the decision as to how to plan for himself less dependent on her availability, although para-doxically he felt she would still want to spend a lot of time doing things together, which he was ambivalent about. Whenever a couple relationship fills the individual sessions I will ask if the other spouse might be invited in. Seth was interested in the idea and shared it with Julie. Julie reported through Seth that she was reluc-tant, because she believed I would be partial to her husband, having seen him for four weeks. However, when she consulted her analyst who said I was good at not taking sides, she was curious to see for herself.

He was a soon-to-be-retiring executive; she had a consulting practice. Seth had been in analytic therapy from forty-two to fifty-two, with an elderly male analyst who focused on his early relation-ship with his father, which included exploring his parents' five-year separation, starting when Seth was five, and ending when his father returned to the family when Seth was ten. An only child, he hated his father for many years but grew to appreciate his father's weak-nesses during the ten years of analytic work. He showed no appre-ciable affect during these early sessions. No dreams had been ana-lyzed, and no work appeared to have been done on his mother issues or the family triangle.

Julie was a wounded child, having been molested by an uncle on her father's side, and in general she felt her family role was to serve men and her rather insensitive mother. She recalled cutting her thigh with a razor blade at age eighteen; this was her way of feeling in touch with her pain, so overlooked in her life. The couple had two daughters (27 and 29) who lived on their own, in another state.

Initial impressions and history revealed a couple who had drifted apart, each living in a separate world of work, with little close communication, although Julie insisted she wanted to be close. Seth preferred Internet pornography; his usage increased as the business came closer to being sold. There was increasing concern for the future. Seth was preoccupied with pornographic photographs of young, slender-built male and female teens and adults; the women were small-boned and small-breasted. Television and Internet pornography were his outlets when at home. He knew it was probably not good for him, but he could not or would not give it up; Julie felt helpless in regard to stopping him.

Julie largely initiated the couple's sex life, and lately Seth was having difficulty maintaining an erection through intercourse, although in individual sessions he said he was as hard as a rock when using the Internet. In a general sense, I felt sad for them. I internally felt they shared an unconscious longing for closeness that was blocked by longstanding individual child-based fears of being re-molested, displaced, and exploited. Neither parent represented a reliable, nurturing object. Julie was the eldest and only girl, with two brothers, the younger being mother's favorite and confidant. Her father had been a powerhouse owner of the company, which Seth married into knowingly, as this was his way of getting a new family and a male parent he could look up to. He initially viewed Julie as a dependent person whom he could take care of, but his motives were primarily driven by the hunger to correct the impoverished childhood yearnings for a father figure whom he could respect and who would guide him.

Prelude to the Dream

In the prior couple session, I had referred to Julie as "your wife" in soliciting her response to Seth's current reference to her as often saying confusing and stupid things, showing an interest in how this may have affected her. Julie had turned to me in a tense and hurt manner and mentioned that I had not called her by name, and she was worried that I could not treat her as an individual, but only could see her as his wife.

The Dream

The dream was Seth's, and it followed my recent request that the couple report any dreams for us to explore in order to enrich the work.

Seth reported that he and Julie went to a foreign country for Andy's bar mitzvah (Andy is the son of Seth's nemesis CEO brother-in-law). In the dream, Andy is not a child. Seth's brother-in-law and soon-to-be-former partner is there and is driving a white BMW. They are in France or Italy (I recognize I drive a white SUV and am Italian). He needs a passport to stop at the border. He is supposed to take public transportation, a train, but has no tokens, and the train does not stop at the border, and he gets into trouble. His brother-in-law tries to purchase two tokens, for sightseeing. Seth gets a passport from a fortune-teller, and a transit worker takes it into the back. He comes back and says, "You are under arrest." If Seth tells the truth and his brother-in-law gets into trouble, or if he lies, how will he meet him in the city they are supposed to meet? Seth does not think he turned in his brother-in-law nor does not he believe he was released after being interrogated.

I asked Seth to comment on what the dream might suggest. He bitterly said that Andy and Julie's youngest brother were recently invited to his brother-in-law's new expensive home on Nantucket, and he was not. He was also approaching his sixtieth birthday and did not want to invite the brother-in-law to his party; in addition, he does not want to go to Andy's actual bar mitzvah but wants to be invited anyway. He was concerned about retiring because he had nothing planned. He had been to a financial planner with Julie recently and worried he would not have the money he planned on because the stock was almost worthless (I had two silent associations: [1] he would be left with a "token" of what he had invested for so many years, and [2] if he seriously "took stock," he would feel worthless). He added, with uncharacteristic animation, that he walked out of a meeting with the perspective buyers, their competitors, after he found out that their employees would be badly compensated if there were a takeover. He expressed rage over the partnership with his brother-in-law ending with an unjust deal. Making the deal pointed to his brother-in-law showing bad character. Seth said that he had a rough night last night and was bitter over getting no support in the past seven years; it did not matter how moral you were, you still get screwed. He said, in a kind of eulogizing way, that Julie was the only member of her family who was not self-centered. She was *bred* to satisfy others.

I turned to Julie, whose mouth was open in disbelief as to what she was hearing. At first, she related that sharing the dream was important to her. She tearfully related that Seth had been anxious last night and would not say anything. She felt that the dream had to do with crossing the boundaries from working to retirement, from being important to the employees who Seth was fair with, to being devalued by the family. She was particularly moved by feeling close to the inside of her husband, an area he never allowed her near. I asked her about Seth's direct comments about her character compared with her brother's. She said Seth always blamed her for the family she came from because he had regarded them as his greatest hope in marrying her.

I wondered about the dream's further meanings. I first commented on the animation; Seth became expressive when discussing being victimized. I offered that he was fighting against being overwhelmed at losing his position of value. I wondered if there were also some sad and lonely parts of him under the rage. I picked up on Julie's idea that boundaries were involved, but I offered the observation that Seth was moving from individual into couple therapy, as was Julie, except she had two different therapists and thus could have separate experiences. Using the language of the dream, and thinking of their individual histories, could they be merely "tokens" of others' uses of them? Another theme was reflected in Seth's paradox of ratting on his brother-in-law and then fearing he would not get to be with him at their destination (I did not say this, but Seth's oedipal history included his mother's confiding in him during his father's long absence that she might remarry; Seth was incensed. To Seth mother's ratting on father meant being mother's only love, and he was on tenuous ground after his father returned home).

I did say that the boundary worries could be about me, as Julie worried about sharing me in a way that would be fair to her in the last session, and this could be Seth's concern about fairness too. How would the therapy reach a good destination? Would I be reliable for each of them? Julie cried and said her mother always referred to her all through life as "my daughter" or "my girl," and not by her first name. She had forgotten that until now.

SOME ADDITIONAL ASSOCIATIONS AND DECIDING WHAT TO DO ABOUT THEM

None of the associations or potential insights I have about a dream would be shared wholesale. I hold them and await the couple's responses, building where possible on the story lines and themes about current or past life, and I particularly look for transference dynamics, related to shared couple anxieties, hopes, or dreads about the therapy. All the while I am tracking each spouse's responses to the dream, as *in vivo* elaborations of resistances or openness to the unknown but slowly emerging internal life of the couple relationship, and I look for revelations of all significant pairings pertaining to the marriage difficulties. I may choose to comment on any dream contents that illustrate developmental threats originating in early childhood or adolescence, and I will discuss in relation to the sexual and emotional conflicts or arrests of either spouse that may be affecting the marriage.

The major technical issue in a new therapy is how to hold, contain, and directly discuss the couple's defenses and anxieties about sharing the therapist; spouses may consciously expect betrayal, favoritism, or being ignored. They may anticipate gender bias, unconsciously fear hostile oedipal rivalry, and harbor deep longings for the dyad. When present, I would select the dream elements that would most effectively promote understanding the threats to trusting each other, to the therapy process, and to me. By highlighting the contextual transferences and empathically relating to them with the couple through the dream, we might detoxify the powerful impediments to collaboration.

WORKING WITH SYMBOLS

Tokens—Transit   Worker—Passport—Getting   Arrested—Bar Mitzvah—Foreign Countries—Borders

If we consider dreams as representing integration, synthesis, and mastery (Fosshage, 1983), they can be viewed as modifications and revelations of psychic process, reflecting reorganization of object relations that are undergoing disorganizing change. Interpersonally, the symbols within the dream may point to attempts at anxiety regulation and can imply preoccupation with defenses. Each spouse may have a stake in these processes while one has the dream experience.

For example, Julie is concerned about whether she is a token in the marriage and perhaps will be in the treatment with me. She is not alone in this, as Seth was comfortable in individual sessions and now has to share me with Julie but is also expected to reveal himself in her presence. He may trivialize the couple sessions and give a token response, preferring to take the role of sightseer (voyeur or expert).

Seth is in a forced retirement, a transition for which he is unprepared. Therapy means getting help, but it also means revealing private dependency conflicts. Hence, the passport is needed but unreliable. Having brother-in-law buy tokens for sightseeing implies a frivolous approach to Seth's concerns about needing a passport to cross the border. This image is related to the business experience and relationship that Seth is so bitter about over the years, in which he was trivialized and bypassed in most company decisions. Getting arrested may mean arrested development during early adolescence in that a bar mitzvah signifies movement into adulthood; if he was forced into a pseudo husband role with his mother, it is accounted for in the dream with Andy in the role as an adult.

There is a perverse narcissistic preoccupation with pornographic websites featuring erotic attractions to early adolescent male and female forms with blurred sexual distinctions; adolescence represents travel to alien/foreign difficult-to-reach countries in order to enter the adult world. The inability to get to the bar mitzvah could be a refusal to enter adult sexuality, as this may be a phobic reaction to overstimulation from his mother prior to adolescence in the five years his father was away from home. Hence, he may be an oedipal victor and terrified of mother-son incest.

For Julie, the dream illustrates that Seth is preoccupied with introjected fears and disowned, abandoned, trivialized, devalued, and degraded self-objects. Julie carries similar feelings about her and seeks to repair Seth through self-sacrifice and trying not to need him too much. Bearing her own suffering characterizes an aspect of how she copes. The dream indicates that Seth is troubled by himself and in relation to male figures, even though there are legitimate hurts and angers at her brother. His sharing the dream and revealing that he had anxieties during the night may lighten

Julie's load and allow her to confront her anger with him instead of falling into depression or abandonment when Seth projects blame into her. On the other hand, she is not in the dream, which may fill her with dread that she may be unimportant in his life except as a salve for his wounded self.

CONCLUDING POINTS

I have illustrated that therapists who are willing to work with the multiple meanings of dream material afford the couple a unique experience within an atmosphere of involved curiosity in how the unconscious world influences couple life and adaptation. Not only are couple dreams apt to enlarge the field of inquiry but their study taps into affects associated with individual and couple projections, and dreams illuminate projective identification in the therapy triangle.

The exceptional position of dreams in our daily work is underscored by the following quote from Freud (1933): "Whenever I began to have doubts of the correctness of my wavering conclusions, the successful transformations of a senseless and muddled dream into a logical and intelligible mental process in the dreamer would renew my confidence of being on the right track" (p. 87).

In this chapter, I expanded the range and application of dream work to couples. I have observed that when couples examine each other's dreams, they potentiate the observing of interpersonal and intrapsychic processes. The uncovering experience of dream reporting and interpretation reduces resistances, and the atmosphere improves for a deeper engagement in cooperative understanding. Freud's method of free association is the cornerstone of dream work and psychoanalysis. We have broadened free association to the couple as a small group. The task of comprehending the dream and its multiple meanings offers the couple and therapist access to individual and couple transferences, here-and-now references to the there-and-then of dynamic histories, and previously hidden traumas and deficits that are frequently disguised in fighting.

Of the many tools available in psychoanalytic practice, I propose that dream work is especially useful in couple, group, and family treatment. The reason why we do not embrace this time-honored tool is a subject for another discussion concerned with contemporary analytic training. Perhaps the influence of hybrid approaches to treatment has put interest in the unconscious to sleep.

When I need reconfirmation of the importance of locating phantasy in myself and my patients, I return to Winnicott (1971) and revisit Klein's (1948) play therapy to appreciate that imagination and imagery are as important in work with adolescents, adults, couples, and families as they are with children. Bion's (1962) beta bits, the sensory experiences lying just beneath the persona, are loaded with primary process, and the patient's psychic retreats are shadowy and full of dread and wonder. They require a safe space to emerge into the interpersonal world for meaning-making and working through. I hope I have created a play space for us to consider analytic work with couples through their dreams. Dream on!

Chapter Eight

The Persecution of Divorce

Instead of being viewed as an unanticipated developmental challenge, divorce has the potential to become a persecutory object both for the partners of a broken marriage and for their couple therapist. Divorcing spouses or partners may torment and persecute each other with their hurt, ambivalence, lost hope, and deep unconscious attachment.

What couple therapist has not agonized over raging couples that struggled over whether to stay together? The couple relationship appears devoid of any good, and yet the partners pursue the forever dream. Fused by hate, loss, disappointment, and betrayal, the partners are unable to detach, or differentiate. They insist on defending themselves righteously against the accusation of the dying marriage and the shared fragmented hope. In a symbiotic partnership or a long marriage with children, the unconscious terror of ending and aloneness are fearful to explore.

Divorce is painful for couple therapists too, even though we are more individuated than the partners in the couple relationship. Their disturbances press hard on us, as we experience the insanity of love gone wrong. Emotion-laden sessions are the usual in working with couples on the brink. But we can use our training to help us deal with loss and dread, and we can think ahead. We can contain our experience. Even so, how we long for the moment after they exit the office, so we can begin our recovery. It is so difficult to help them let go.

We need concepts to help us to contain the potentially devastating effects of the fallout of a failed relationship. With little preparation from training and scant information in the literature, we are challenged to keep our heads clear and our egos intact when feeling persecuted during such difficult work. The lack of theory follows from an avoidance of thinking about the therapist's pain and suffering that is to be expected in terminations of all types. In dealing with the regression inherent in the divorcing couple we find ourselves quite alone when we need the most support.

Termination anxiety accompanies work with a terminal marriage, and it affects the therapist and the couple. Fear of the end of a marriage brings harshness to the therapy process. Angry protest precedes acceptance, which cannot be arrived at without going through a mourning process.

Mourning the lost marriage is difficult to do with the spouse who is about to be lost, and with the couple therapist who is also about to become a lost object. The pain is often too great for the couple to stay with the therapist they originally chose as the one they hoped could help them save their marriage. Too few couples in a divorce mode stay long enough to grieve their loss so as to move on to individual lives with confidence and understanding of their vulnerabilities.

In cases of divorce, loss of love brings with it a cruel and persecutory superego. Persecutory anxieties emerge from spouses who are in pain. Unprepared for dealing with the unimagined demise of their wished-for marriage, a couple feels pain and persecutory anxiety. Suddenly the parting spouses have to learn skills they did not expect to need. They need reworking in therapy to adapt to dashed expectations and prepare for the future. Some couple are so damaged by the time they get to the therapist that they cannot undertake the therapy task. With others we aim to help them rework the malignant projective matrix. The goal of therapy is to help each partner mourn the loss of the good and bad parts of the marriage and re-own the parts of the self that had been projected into the spouse.

Some couples arrive for treatment obviously at the brink of marital dissolution. The verbal attacks are dramatic, unrelenting, violent, and sometimes irrational. Yet, hard work sometimes salvages the relationship, much to our surprise. Other couples are rational and cooperative. We may think that such a couple will respond well in therapy, only to find out that this type of couple is one step from indifference, a death knell for marriage. Detachment of affect implies an emotional separation of long duration without a formal notice. Love is indeed gone. Some couples present when one spouse emphasizes the other's vulnerable personality. The more "sick" individual is placed in our care for the day when the complaining spouse vacates the home, and the therapy. Other couples initially appear to be very much intact, with just a few problems to be worked with, but as therapy goes forward a deeper malignancy emerges when one spouse begins to change for the better. The new behavior is unfamiliar and it disturbs the projective identificatory system of the marriage. We may be shocked to see the marriage deteriorate right before us, no matter how Herculean our efforts.

When there is individual growth in one spouse's ability to relate and be intimate, the other spouse experiences an unwelcome jolt in the system. The integrity of the unconscious object relations set of the marriage has now been disrupted. An unexpected new good experience in treatment creates a deep disturbance, as there is now the possibility of reliable dependency. Massive schizoid defenses are mobilized against it. When one spouse becomes self directed and self-defining as a more whole object, the borderline spouse is torn apart with envy and attacks the possibility of integration. Further individual breakdown then sabotages movement into the depressive position. In other couples, the spouse who longed for improvement in the partner and finally gets it cannot accept it because of resentment at how long it took. Sometimes change is too little or too late. Sometimes hope is too painful to bear, for fear of renewed disappointment.

CLINICAL ILLUSTRATION: ANNE AND BOB

Anne called in deep distress. She told me that she had been married to Bob for thirty-five years, and that they are the parents of three successful grown children. Three weeks ago, she said, Bob announced he wanted out of the marriage. The first hint of this came four months ago while purchasing furnishings for a new home in Florida. One day Bob said he was unhappy. Anne was in shock, became highly emotional, tearful, and hysterical, and Bob backed off. She said that this time Bob hasn't backed off, in fact he seems so much in a hurry to get out she wondered if he had someone else.

Now on the phone, Anne is close to being out of control. She tells me she is frightened, desperate, clutching herself to hold herself together, her entire existence at stake. All her life she has been taken care of by Bob. They have been everything to each other, since she was fifteen, he eighteen. They have done everything together—child rearing, business failures and great successes, and now this, an earthquake. She needs help. She says she is willing to do anything to save the marriage and will come in immediately. I ask if Bob will come too. Since they got my name for her, she is sure he will be motivated to come in to "help her get therapy for the marriage." Anne shows no awareness of the implications of stating Bob's motives in this way.

I schedule Bob and Anne as an emergency that evening. Bob is self-assured, in control, calm and articulate. Anne is wide-eyed, high-strung, and painfully tearful form the start, obviously in shock. Bob restates what Anne has related on the phone: he is there for her, he wants to help her through this, but that he has reached a decision and wants to move things along as soon as possible.

"Why so fast?" I ask.

"Because I am fifty-six years old and I don't want to waste time. I still love Anne and I know she is a good person, but I don't want to be married to her anymore."

This sounds as if Bob is simply dealing with a solution to his personal anxiety over aging, as if it had nothing to do with Anne or the quality of their marriage. So, I inquire about prior marital problems in this long marriage. Anne reveals she had an affair twelve years ago. When Bob found out about this he felt persecuted by the images of her involvement with another man and he became violently disturbed. They went together for counseling. After only two sessions they left with the advice to try and get past it. They tell me they never spoke of it again. I note they are talking about it now with me, in the first session of this, the next treatment opportunity. I ask how they could avoid talking about such an important sign of trouble since then until now. Calmer now, Anne volunteers that there was no sex in the affair: She got to the motel but she couldn't go through with it. Sex wasn't the primary motive for her. I nod for her to continue. Bob is staring at her. She looks away, then at Bob, and tells me sadly that he never believed that she didn't have sex. Bob chuckles at this and says that sex was one of the problems in the marriage. Anne firmly blocks him, defensively pressing that we was so tired with work problems she thought he needed to sleep. I ask if they differed on other issues, or needs in the marriage, and any other disturbances they never got past.

They continue telling me about their roles in the marriage—he the financial provider and protector, she the home-based provider and child-rearing parent. Anne tearfully relates she has no other skills, that she is nothing without Bob! He answers with a limp reassurance that she will be okay, because they can sell the house, and the settlement should be quick and easy. I am thinking to myself that he hasn't heard her at all. I ask Anne if she is ready for such discussions or decisions. She responds that the room is spinning, this is so fast. I intervene saying to Bob that if he insists on going this fast harm may be done and a backlash may follow. He nods, saying he can see how upset Anne is. I ask if there is anyone else in his life that he might be in a hurry to be with. I was taking my cue from something on the phone Anne had said about him moving so fast that she believes there is another woman. Anne says she has received an anonymous phone call telling her Bob has a woman in Dallas. Anne says she confronted him, but he denied it with a story about a business enemy trying to make trouble.

I look at Bob waiting for him to answer my loaded question. He doesn't look at me. He doesn't answer. I ask if they believe there might be room for reconciliation, or if not, could they agree to a slowing down of the separation process, while we all think about what led to their current crisis and they can have time to adjust to the changes. Bob says he will come if it will help Anne, but he insists that he wants out of the marriage. He remains calm, self-centered, and adamant. I tell them that "coming to therapy for Anne" will lead to ending the marriage. Would Anne benefit from this format? Anne does not respond to my comment on the meaning of conjoint sessions from Bob's point of view, but she says she wants to come back. I close the session by mentioning that thirty-five years together means that much has transpired and needs to be reviewed, and that each of their futures depended on learning as much as possible about themselves in the relationship. We could determine whether they could accomplish this together, or not, in which case individual therapy would be a good option.

I wanted to assess if this was going to be marriage therapy or divorce therapy, a consult to determine individual therapy needs, or no basis for therapy at all. Based on Bob's attitude, I felt little optimism that they could use couple therapy to recover their marriage, or that Bob would accept individual therapy, but I hoped to slow him down a bit. Bob experienced this offer of sessions as an opportunity for relieving himself of a guilty burden and getting on with his life. Anne saw it as an opportunity to prevent the fragmentation of her self, and perhaps to change Bob's mind. My approach offered time, space, and a holding environment in which Anne might be able to confront the enormity of her plight, or at least reduce the immediacy of her impending loss, and Bob could review his decision without causing a panic. I might be allowed to help them detoxify the persecutory effects of Bob's lack of sexual desire, Anne's old affair, and the threat of divorce itself.

Guilt and fear complicate the decision to divorce. A spouse may worry that the spouse being left will break down, or become so livid that violence might ensue in the form of suicide, or destructive legal attacks. Here the persecutory superego exerts its wrath over the lost love object (Schecter, 1979). The ego is under attack and previous holding that was good enough in the long marriage is unable to sustain a more benign adjustment to its termination. The dependent wife cannot rely on her husband any more except to the extent that there is a legal provision for her. If the husband was the ego ideal, the wife being left can no longer count on association to him to maintain her self-esteem. When the fears of loss of income, loss of companionship, loss of social standing, and loss of self-esteem are intense, narcissistic clinging of one spouse to the other may last for months or years. Even after a legal separation and divorce the persistence of this phenomenon cannot be underestimated.

THE BABY AS SAVIOR

Dick and Maggie had been unhappy in a childless marriage of twenty-four years. They had been in marital therapy for two years without improvement in how they felt. Termination of the marriage and of treatment seemed inevitable when it became gradually and mutually clear how little they had in common to work with toward reconciliation. Maggie no longer loved Dick. Nevertheless, she insisted that he give her a baby, even though significant marital problems had not been worked through, including her infidelities, his difficulty in providing financially for the two of them, much less a child, and their couple intimacy and sexual issues. Dick refused to provide her with the necessary sperm.

Within three months of moving out, Maggie showed up unannounced at the couple's former residence demanding custody of the two dogs. Dick agreed to her having visitation once a week but he resented her request being made in this intrusive way. She took the opportunity to tell him that she would return to the marriage, if he would relent and give her the baby she required. Dick's life was beginning to take shape, while Maggie's was bogged down in continuing anxiety, and insecurity, and a desperate longing to have life from the man she could not love.

AT THE EX-SPOUSE'S SERVICE

Tony had moved out of the home he had shared with his wife, Alice. After the separation, Tony continued out of guilt and curiosity to be available to help Alice prepare and physically set up her art shows, work for which she had no motivation during the marriage. Alice had lost considerable weight, partly from depression associated with his moving out, but it suited her and she looked well. She was working out for the first time in her life, she was productive, and her outlook was improved. Previously so dependent when married, Alice was now on her way to a new life without Tony. Her individuation was felt as a psychic injury to him. It turned out that Tony had wanted a life with a younger woman, more lively and self-directed in contrast to Alice. His disillusionment with his marriage had led to a long-term affair that increased his withdrawal and further fuelled Alice's depression. Their relationship had clearly been unfulfilling over many years and Tony's decision to end the marriage was final.

Although there was little evidence of love and devotion between them from the earliest days of the marriage, Tony continued, for some time after the separation, to cling to Alice in the role of her assistant. This was partly due to his awe of her needing him less, and his difficulty in giving up the role as parental caregiver. What they shared, even after the divorce, was the unconscious long-term assumption that the only form of couple relationship was one consisting of an anaclitic, infantile dependency, with the parent and child roles oscillating between them. Fearful of individuation, they looked after each other, but without passion or growth potential.

THE FOLLY OF FORGIVENESS

Rachel, a thirty-year-old woman in a three-year marriage to Saul, eventually separated from him after two years of marital therapy. She suffered through to the realization that she had married him to please her family. Her hysterical, somatic symptoms worsened as she got closer to her divorce as if the clamor in her body could no longer be quieted by her association with him. Although not an abusive person, Saul nevertheless represented the abuse that Rachel had not been allowed to protest. His presence in the family calmed her parents just as she had previously. Her marital and childhood roles overlapped. She was to keep the peace between her spouse and herself, and this paralleled the feared-based childhood in which she had colluded with her father to ignore and forgive the emotional and physical abuse heaped on her by her mother and older sister. Keeping her father's love required Rachel's constant forgiveness of her family. In her teens when she recognized that her father was desperately depressed, Rachel felt burdened with guilt, and continued protecting her parents at the sacrifice of her own needs.

Rachel had picked Saul, because he was a nice, cute, Jewish accountant who was adored by her family. He didn't abuse her, but he neglected her needs and withdrew from her demands as her father had done. Her fantasy marriage quickly evaporated, with the result that the neglect and withholding of the past were repeated in the relationship. After the separation there was tremendous pressure on Rachel to forgive Saul, to see only his good points, and to re-unite with him. On the one hand Saul asked Rachel for forgiveness (a stunning reversal of the childhood pattern), but on the other hand he continued to manipulate her emotionally and sided with her parents who obviously preferred him to her. The therapist was also pressured by phone calls from the mother requesting him to bring the therapy to a happy ending, by getting the daughter to give up her crazy ideas and forgive her husband. To Rachel's credit she worked through the painful dynamics and moved ahead, but the family's malignant projective matrix continued to require her to give them absolution. Understanding the family dynamics from work done in the marital therapy, Rachel became much sturdier in meeting the challenge of maintaining her autonomy.

Few situations are as challenging or persecuting for couples and for therapists as the issue of divorce. It draws into the consulting room our personal value system concerning monogamy, what makes marriage work, and what undermines it. When faced with the possibility of the end of a marriage our countertransference may be concordant with the feelings of the children. We fear our parents' failing us, or we grieve for our failure to keep them together. The painful prospect of being involved in a great loss stirs us to the core. Our psychoanalytic paradigm is no insurance against this. Simply tracing each spouse's unconscious precursors of marital conflict and making the unconscious conscious are not sufficient as therapeutic approaches. We have to use object relations theory applied to the interpersonal situation of the couple relationship. Working with here and now realities in marriage is not necessarily collusion with defenses against exploring the past. It is as important as dealing with past traumas, neglect, and failed attachments that have influenced premarital life and mate choices. Such issues as hope, subculture, religion, devotion, will, loyalty, and spirituality need to be included when we are exploring couple resilience and potential for reworking the relationship.

We ask couples to what extent is there a narcissistic preoccupation with the self and its right to be served by the spouse. Is personal sacrifice seen as a restriction of individual needs and strivings? To what extent are communal issues, or the needs of the group, including the family, a major concern for one or the other spouse? The balance between the needs of the individual, the marriage, the nuclear family, and the families of origin is central to the future of the marital institution itself. In one case keeping the family together was the driving force for the husband to remain married, due to his ethnic and cultural values. The wife was not of his background and could have taken the action leading to divorce, but she had accommodated to his views about family values. Shame was a powerful motive for maintaining this loveless marriage.

The literature abounds with discussion of the effects of divorce on children of different ages, the legal ramifications, the economic impact, the problems of remarriage and blending families, and the reactions of extended family members and friends. Not so available to us especially in the psychoanalytic literature are the interpersonal and intrapsychic aspects of marital dissolution, the shared object relations that must be deconstructed in a divorcing process, and

discussion of the therapist's role in the process of growth and recovery. How does the couple therapist cope when one or both of
the spouses do not recover after the marriage fails?

Perhaps our literature lacks details of these phenomena because
of the clinician's pain in studying and staying with the lingering
process of marital dissolution. Being so close to couples puts us
uncomfortably close to their loss and sense of failure. We may feel
like ejecting them from treatment under pressure from our internal
objects if our losses are linked to the affects of the couple's loss.
Each of us has personal and professional feelings that color the
extent to which we can approach the object relations of divorce. We
may not have mastered all these feelings, but we can work with
them if we feel supported. Too few analytic therapists come together to discuss and explore these issues, and so there is not a good
containing environment in which therapists can find help with processing their experience.

Since divorce is a form of termination, an understanding of loss
and mourning may be of help in contemplating the end of a marriage and the end of a couple's treatment. In his paper "Mourning
and Melancholia" Freud (1917) described the process of acceptance
of loss at times of grief: "Each single one of the memories and
situations of *expectancy* which demonstrates the libido's attachment to the lost object is met by the verdict of *reality* that the object
no longer exists; and the ego, confronted as it were with the question of whether it shall share this fate, is persuaded by the sum of
the narcissistic satisfactions it derives from being alive to sever its
attachment to the object it has abolished" (p. 255).

In her paper "A Contribution to the Psychogenesis of Manic-
Depressive States," Klein (1935) wrote that the loss of good objects
is a major threat to our security, and fear of this loss is the source of
great pain and conflict. Alteration in the external circle of family
objects produces insecurity in the internal objects. Threats to good
internal objects leave the child feeling filled up with bad, persecu-

tory objects and fears of annihilation of the self. Depending on the nature of the internal objects children and adults can experience manic and depressive responses to anxiety. These anxieties are related to phantasies and affects associated with the internalized mother colored by whether she was experienced as helpful or revengeful, loving or angry.

During our development as therapists we have internalized objects based on our experiences with our own internal mothers, our teachers, our therapists, and former clients. These internal objects have attributes that may be dangerous and unpleasant or consistent and helpful. Dealing with divorce in couple therapy, we are faced with mainly the more dangerous and unpleasant ones. We experience sorrow, distress, and feelings associated with failure such as low self-esteem arising from perceptions of ourselves as unhelpful objects.

Any leave-taking regenerates loss and mourning issues for us (Martin and Schurtman, 1985). Even the cases that we wish would leave treatment cause us pain, since we feel persecuted by our own hate of a particular couple or divorcing partner. We feel guilty to be relieved of the burden of some couples. We are alive, witnessing a death, even though a necessary one if the individual spouses are to develop by beginning anew. If so much of marriage is dependent on a search for lost objects, then when that marriage breaks up, it becomes another lost object compounding a previous, and perhaps deeper, loss. What was never achieved in the marriage cannot be recovered in the marriage, or in the divorce.

During the divorcing process, infantile loss and the painful layering of reactions to frustrated hopes are experienced again. Conscious and unconscious attachments are severed for a second time. No wonder couples often fly into manic attempts to salvage what they can. The denial of psychic reality allows the attachment to persist in the face of tremendous difficulty. In despair, a spouse may become depressed with suicidal feelings, while the other may act out through extramarital flight. Murder or suicide end growth for spouses dramatically, but more commonly unresolved grief cripples future growth in an ordinary way. Defenses including omnipotence, avoidance, even idealization may continue to prevent total collapse and assuage one spouse's terror of the depressive position.

If we have too much anxiety about endings and losing divorcing couples from treatment we may rush them into premature endings. On the other hand, we may deter them from making the decision to end the marriage by rehashing marriage dynamics ad nauseum to avoid blaming ourselves for incipient abandonment of the couple. We may have difficulty letting the spouses leave each other and us if our self-esteem is insecure. Our professional competence is shaken by termination due to unanticipated divorce if we are not always prepared for that eventuality, even though we should be because we know that it is not our responsibility to save marriages or to break them up. We simply help couples learn, and they are ultimately responsible for the fate of their relationship. Yet, in the throes of flawed couple relating, we may be drawn into an attempt to improve holding so that we do not face the narcissistic injury of not being able to help the couple hold on to their commitment. We may seek object constancy in the face of object sorting and splitting in the couple. In this phase of therapy the splitting may be a necessary part of dissolution of the marriage partnership and we must learn to accept it.

It is painful for us to recognize that as we succeed in our approach, the couple fails in the marriage. The loss of a meaningful relationship with this couple can cause a crisis of confidence in our professional life. We may obsess over the case. Have we done all we could? Do we ever know for sure? We may turn against ourselves through self-deprecation, self-abasement, or depression. We wonder, question, analyze our reactions, and if necessary seek consultation to ensure that we maintain an impartial sensitivity to the needs of both the divorcing partners.

I continue to be amazed at the need for personal growth and accommodation to reality that divorcing couples force upon me. I have to admit that I do not always welcome the variety of experiences I have to contend with in the pursuit of a therapeutic ending. I am forced to face the worked through and unworked through parts of my internal world as the loss of love reaches its emotional peak. The struggle between the benign and persecutory elements in the object relations of divorcing clients evokes the therapist's own struggles. The couples shame, guilt, and low self-esteem resonate with our own. The divorcing partners may regress and attempt to kill off what was once loved and that may include annihilating us. If hatred of the object and splitting instead of ambivalence dominate the separation process, hate will not then be available to the self for use in differentiation, separation, new realistic boundary setting, and mourning loss. Instead the hated spouse or therapist takes on an entirely bad persona to preserve the self as good. This is a precarious bargain since the distribution of all-good and all-bad can shift, and then suddenly it is the self that feels bad. Splitting in which only good or bad can be tolerated at one time leads to destructive actions alternately toward the self and the formerly loved partner. While these dynamics frequently accompany divorce to some degree they usually resolve over time to a more mature state of ambivalence.

In object relations dominated by persecutory superego functioning that has not been resolved in therapy, the therapist notes with regret that the primitive and punitive affects will continue to affect individual and family development long after the divorce is final. This knowledge propels us to keep divorcing couples in therapy long enough for them to learn as much as possible about themselves and the nature of the relationship they created so that mistakes in fit are not repeated. Sensitivity to the client's capacity to endure this type of soul-searching is essential so that we judge correctly the moment when enough is enough. Otherwise the result will be abandonment of treatment, rather than a mature integration of the feelings of love and hate, with resolved grief over past losses and hope for an easier future. Comfort with the therapeutic process of the divorcing couple is at best a momentary accomplishment. Detoxifying the persecutory object of divorce is not an easy matter, but it can be achieved through applying learning about termination anxiety, tolerating the persecutory superego affects, and metabolizing the attacks on our loving selves. We may add to the outcome of our efforts a mature forgiveness of ourselves when some marriages, and some treatments, inevitably fail.

Chapter Nine

Containment, Projective Process, and the Couple

The Therapist's Dream

The practice of couple therapy has adapted fundamental ideas from Winnicott's (1986) contribution on the *holding environment* of the "good-enough mother" combined with Bion's (1961) theory of the *container-contained* relationship. Each contribution describes an intrapsychic-interpsychic (self-to-other reciprocity) interpersonal structure—a mother-infant paradigm of optimal emotional attunement; one feature is the ability of the "environmental mother" to mentalize, imagine, and intuit correctly what the infant is clamoring for but cannot use language to make known. In the treatment setting I conceptualize the holding environment as the provision of a space within a frame that replicates the mother-infant dyad and does not impinge on the baby's safe exploration of the world, including his body ("psychosomatic partnership") (note contextual transference). The material environment (nursery or clinical setting) is assumed to be safe and comfortable; by safe we mean no sharp or scary objects.

The second feature is the mother/therapist's ability to mentalize what is intuited through *reverie* (empathy, compassion, sympathy, and love) and to physically and emotionally respond in comforting the baby when in distress and returning it to a steady state; the loving mother/therapist offers the baby other objects (object mother) including herself. Assuming a sufficiently consistent repetition of attunement, developmental supplies become internalized as self structure, building a template for becoming a self in the world. When the process of informed nurturing is interrupted (whether by high anxiety, poor fit, depression, environmental catastrophe, or other traumas), disruptions in self-and-other relating can lead to maladaptive object relations. Individuals with impaired object relations marry a partner with similar maladaptive tendencies; hence the couple container cannot contain.

To the Winnicott/Bion paradigms, we add triadic thinking by expanding the treatment dyad to a field of three—husband, wife and therapist. The goal of triadic thinking is to comprehend the effects on containment in relation to the therapist and the couple. Couple disturbances cause therapist disturbance; when stimulated by ego-alien transferences, his containment may be interrupted or shut down due to counter-projections or emotional anesthesia. With difficult couples we guard against imitating an image of the therapist in favor of internalizing the frame and linking our idiom to it so as to become a therapist.

1. In the clinical setting, *containment* refers to affective-mental processing of states of mind in relationships. It is often misunderstood as merely offering a calming effect when emotions run high.
2. Containment can be misguided therapeutic masochism and empathy may turn into mind control over the patient's self-serving eagerness to be "understood"—as in remaining the same (narcissistic defenses against change).

3. In the interpersonal sense, containment becomes expected and is transparent. This is reflected in the material comfort of the setting, the therapist's listening stance, tone of voice, and concern for the couple's well-being.
4. Contemporary approaches to containment involve therapist expressiveness and spontaneity, which join with interpretive and invisible affective tolerance.

MASCULINE AND FEMININE SYMBOLS AND CONTAINER-CONTAINED

Bion (1963) gave us the symbols of male and female in representing the container-contained. Masculine-feminine phenomenal counterparts operate as expressions in material reality representing P/S (paranoid-schizoid) or depressive couple positions (Klein, 1948). In therapy sessions we observe couple interactions based on a feminine and masculine apprehension of the fertile couple. An optimal intercourse of the male and female contribution consists of the intuitive, loving, caring part that functions as a receptive environment; creating a baby propitiates a partnership capable of grasping something real and alive. The masculine part is motivated to do things and to penetrate, protect, and present material reality. The session produces each partner's pursuit of and frustrated attempts at psychic potency, and the frame offers an opportunity to generate meanings not merely rooted in the intellectual or rational dimension of the masculine. The idea of a creative couple blends the desires for procreation with potency, giving life and protecting life. Psychoanalytic therapy has many features of the feminine—think again about Winnicott's (1956) *primary maternal preoccupation:* caring, creating, and connecting. Therapy penetrates, by interpreting flights from new experience illustrating the masculine element. Containment seen from this perspective topples icons and subverts the tolerable by creating new tensions in the couple's syntonic patterns of relating. With couples promoting curiosity is a profoundly disturbing therapist ambition. Instead of dominance and submission we offer affiliation and self-reflection. If the pain of therapy is tolerated better than the pain of living there can be containment. Containment from this perspective offers hope!

The therapist is not a passive or objective participant. Due to the interest in unconscious process he sits poised on the boundary between the couple and himself; although he may naively view the work from the neck up it is the *body* (mind-body sensibility) of the clinical experience and the feminine approach that shapes his understanding. As a player in the field, the therapist is as susceptible as the couple to object and subject oscillations (transference enactments). The therapist therefore has a ready-for-use pool of object relations.

I am proposing an expanded unconscious field that can produce *mutual containment* as well as noncontainment enactments. Meaning-making and attacks on meaning-making are common unconscious occurrences, which involve the susceptible therapist. Being in the triad typifies movement from the D to P/S position. Transferences move about, interconnected by an *unthought known* (Bollas, 1987), meaning yesterday's definers of reality may become today's new symbols by comparison.

In Winnicott's terms, the *transitional space* permits meaning through metaphor, a play of ideas, images and suggestions. But the battle for meaning-making between the three minds in the field is won and lost in each session to the degree that containment fails. Can we endure feeling lost and helpless and recover our reflective capacities? Ambivalence is associated with the paradox of marital intimacy and individual solitude, often observed as a split. Regressive pulls accompany disruptions caused by therapist comments; mother transferences strike fear in the couple if the comments are received as intrusion, trauma, or negative affects. When faced with couples for whom splitting unwanted parts of self and other is a preferred mode of relating therapist flexibility in thinking about interpsychic collusion may be compromised. Enactments result and the hope is for a recovery of therapist reflective capacities so there can be a shift from the concrete to a transformative process.

ADDITIONAL FEATURES OF CONTAINMENT

Containment is transitory and amplifies a piece of what is there or not there, revealing a concealment of unsecured truth. In learning about what is known and not known we need a psychological structure that processes unconscious and conscious experience. The containment factor plays a large part in determining object relations and preserving the abilities to exist on the boundary between internal references that distort meanings and to process external influences. Reverie provides the betweenness of individuality and connection to the universe of otherness. Moving from a symbiosis (oneness) to more differentiated experience (as one human to another) is the greatest challenge to identity formation. Transference manifests problems in identity formation and reveals the maladaptive couple containment process that we have to discover by repeating aspects of it as willing recipients. In some respects containment functions differently from holding. Containment requires verbal activity linked to affective disturbances and discharge. We cannot, for example reduce the fear of violence through the dimming of office lighting or providing more comfortable furniture. A hands-on use of self is called for when suicide is spoken about, depressed despair emerges, or an embezzlement or secret affair is discovered.

All psychic experience emerges from the absent, or "no breast," as in alpha-functioning—thinking new thoughts, for example. Transference prevents separateness. The creative illusion of transference is enacted with the therapist; transferences are transported from the marriage to the triad. The triad consists of:

1. My past—their present (T)—A convergence of incongruity.
2. Their past—my present (CT). Each participant transmits container-contained interrelationship patterns; the therapist's task is to unmask central aspects of what and who is hiding beneath transferences.
3. My past—their past (Multi-Ts) (deeper unmetabolized contained-container issues). The lack of a container to contain the triad.

With regressed couples, narcissistic injuries consist of "no-breast" abandonment—an inability to be alone in the presence of another. Borderlines disregard preconceptions because psychic conflict is too threatening. Absence can mean a breakdown—meaning one cannot mate with a realization of an inner breast to match an expectation of reverie—comfort and hope. Patients seek comfort but without hope.

In a triad, the relationships are viewed as the container; that means more than the sum of the individuals. The field consists of psychic dimensions, depth, levels of pain, and (unmodified and modified) projections, and the field contains libidinal and antilibidinal motives.

CONTAINMENT WHEN A PARTNER IS SEEN IN SEPARATE SESSIONS WITHIN COUPLE TREATMENT

A partner seen in individual sessions may exhibit different and fewer symptoms, defenses, and projective elements due to the dyad. Is this desirable, and what might be the consequences for couple work? What are the other partner's phantasies and transferences to being excluded, and would the individual sessions cause the couple to think one partner is the more disturbed, relieving the other to scapegoat or justified blaming? What does the therapist do with the information and experience with the dyad? Is it "confidential"? Can aspects of it be applied in the couple sessions?

Place the two partners within the couple container, and the more repressed side blossoms. The unbearable parts emerge more fully in plain sight. The couple container is more evident when in the triad because the sharing of the therapist causes regression—competition, sibling issues, and longings to be the only child easily show up. The marital container more easily tips us off to the fundamentals of couple fit. To return to the therapy dyad, transference elements will be present; however, couple-centered projections may not readily surface due to more optimal therapist holding. Core couple affective issues may lie under the surface in individual sessions because the partner is not present to trigger them.

THE COUPLE CASE

Note: I chose the names based on the old TV comedy show Mork and Mindy, *which was about a young couple in which the male (Robin Williams) was an alien from the planet Ork who looked like a human and tried to adapt to his new planet, and his partner (Pam Dawber) was an earthling. It was on the air 1978–1982. The odd couple married in the final season.*

Mork is forty-eight, Mindy forty-six. They came to see me eight months ago after Mindy discovered Mork's telephone bills and became suspicious about his recent trip to another city where a former neighbor of theirs in her second marriage now resides. She reported that he had been withdrawn and noncommunicative. After she confronted Mork with her suspicions, he became angry that she had gone through his bills. They argued about what the truth was, and after Mork relented he had a secret relationship, she called around for a couple therapist, which Mork reluctantly accepted, saying he wanted to move forward.

Description

Mork, a high-ranking CFO, was tall—6'4", slender, and built like a basketball player. Mindy was about 5'8" with an expressive face and dark brown hair. My early impressions were not favorable as to a working alliance due to his secretive position—he would not discuss or answer Mindy's questions at home or in the early sessions about what was going on with the other woman, for how long, or on what level. Betrayal was at the center of her feelings. I felt I was there initially to allow Mindy to vent and to interrogate Mork. My sense of why he was there took the form of a split; I thought by his glances he needed my protection, but he didn't trust me at all. He confronted (by direct questioning) my policy on taking sides in these matters. I said my job was to understand the relationship and how they got into the current mess. I initially told them that the fallout of betrayal was in the room and wondered if they given thought to what contributed to it?

Mindy was a top architect in a real estate development company and was used to being in charge. She had to know what she was up against. Mork insisted that the former neighbor was not a threat to the marriage, although he admitted having seen her in person three times while on business trips, but only in friendship and to advise her on money matters. He insisted he loved and was faithful to Mindy. He just needed a friend over the years because he did not have any from childhood. He further insisted he had no intention of giving up the relationship, and Mindy should not be jealous. I asked why the relationship was kept a secret if there was nothing to fear. Mork got my point and hinted he had not thought of that, but he was adamant about how harmless it was.

The beginning encounter highlighted the split in the marriage and in the initial sessions. Rather than pressing further into Mork's defenses and passively witnessing Mindy's meltdown, I decided to address the couple's motives for seeking help, trying to determine if the pain of the crisis would be enough motivation to keep them in therapy. There was little room in the early going to offer Mindy any intervention that would offer comfort, and Mork was attempting damage control by minimizing his need for the outside relationship. Instead I asked if they would be willing to come for awhile given the circumstances and to discuss the marriage in light of the break-down of trust. What got them to continue was that Mindy was clear that she was prepared to leave the marriage as long as Mork remained shut down. Being that Mork could not trust Mindy to stay married to him, he agreed to come for awhile but was clearly against therapy.

For several months, the couple oscillated between Mork's limited "remorse" and a go-forward approach, as in asking me directly what he could do to gain Mindy's trust, given Mindy's insistence that he had to come clean or else she could never trust him. She was in pain and was quite desperate. Reading his mind took hold of her, and his every moment away from home was questioned by jealous outrage. Mork's narcissistic web of deceit was peeling slightly, albeit stemming from an infantile superego.

He began to show good faith by calling Mindy frequently, especially when out of town, buying her gifts, and once doing the laundry; this is how he asked for forgiveness and vowed his telephone/ e-mail relationship was over. He also owned up on a more troubled aspect of the deceit with the other woman: He had involved his daughter in a match-making attempt at the ex-secretary's invitation with her son, citing that his daughter was shy and needed some social experience. The woman's son was also shy. I was reminded of the earlier session when Mork pleaded for understanding that he needed friends; now he was acting out that deficit, held within himself by taking on the love life of the younger male and projecting his own neediness into his daughter. He asked the daughter to remain silent as well, thus compounding the betrayal. As the gory story grew, Mork's daughter spoke with her older sister, resulting in the two daughters turning against him; their boundaries had been violated by father's hunger to heal his old wounds, and they refused to be in the middle. Accountability for this breech of family boundaries came at a high price, as Mindy's new regard (which Mork had recently earned) took a second hit.

Though sessions were incendiary, we cautiously continued the work through this difficult time. The couple was able to hold together, and more background material emerged. Both partners were chosen to carry responsibility for meeting their parents' wishes. Although they had siblings, they still had the major responsibilities for the care and financial well-being of their parents. Each partner was able to express hurt and (later) anger at not getting recognition for their "goodness," having taken themselves for granted, just as their parents had (a subject behaving as the persecuting object pertains to unconscious identifications with the aggressor by repeating what was done to them). With the mothers, it was: "Do for us what we want because we took care of you as a child. Now you owe us." Gathering this new material indirectly opened up what the couple unconsciously projectively identified with. Unconscious obligations to family had taken a toll because they received no appreciation for their family sacrifices. The marriage was repeating a sadomasochistic element not previously known to the couple: Sacrifice and loyalty was breaking down in the marriage while the child-based obligations to parents and the accompanying resentments for being used had remained underground. Mork felt he was entitled to have the outside "friendship," and Mindy was waking up to her part of the history of being taken for granted. At first, she focused only on Mork. Eventually they mutually discovered that they both carried repressed anger over being used in childhood.

I will now turn to a specific element of containment in the couple case in which a mutual containment provided hope for the treatment when my containment capacities were under siege.

A therapist dream to illustrate a struggle with containment:

Mr. Myogi sat across from the couple—Mork sat to his left and Mindy on the right, looking at the trouser seam along his left thigh. A one-inch opening had lost stitching and appeared just the right size, had he wished to place his index finger in it. It would fill the space exactly, and had he inserted a finger, it could have been removed easily. At that moment, he looked up at Mork's face. It was distorted; specifically, the forehead and eyes were much larger than the cheeks, nose, lips, and chin. These protruding features reminded him of a Neanderthal, just now realizing he had not been empathizing with Mork throughout the couple treatment. Mork looked at him through beady eyes, Mr. Myogi noted; up came a familiar feeling that Mork could not see beyond his thick skull. Trying to empathize had not worked, and he was giving up on trying, as though empathy was an intrusion. Better if he connected with the negative feelings Mork was evoking and see where that led. Mr. Myogi listened once again as Mork repeated to his wife and to me that no harm was intended in his ten-year "telephone relationship" with the former secretary who left his office suddenly twenty-six years ago without notice. He reported that she needed his help from time to time; that was all. Mr. Myogi self-consciously put his finger into the small space along the seam and left it there, wondering if Mork or Mindy could see it. At that moment, he felt he wanted to open it more along the seam, while simultaneously thinking that he was too preoccupied with it and wanting to sew it up. Mindy became tearful and angry, as though on cue, and Mork looked over at Mr. Myogi—something spoke in Mork's eyes, a glimpse of sadness perhaps.

Analysis of the Dream

I was in a state of imbalance, with strong negative affect at play. I felt fear and anger about containing Mork—I could not live in a world of his severe denial, or moral deadness; I felt drawn into Mork's insatiable entitlement; an infantile realm of hostile dependency that breeds pragmatic trade-offs—"I pay the bills, you allow me freedom to act out a perverse fantasy." Self-justification was used as a thick skin in keeping me out while forcing me into one way of thinking—rationalizing; from my standpoint I was split (with or against him). I could not empathize with him, although I was interested in the way in which he placed his marriage in such jeopardy—he seemed naïve. The effect on me was a *claustrum* (Meltzer, 1967)—the experience of a couple psychic envelope so compact that one can get out of it only by force. I did, however, empathize with Mindy as the victim of his neediness. Mindy captured my imagination, raising questions about her complex motives. She is in some ways like him—sacrificial, independent—except she is more indirect. She saves up frustrations and later blows up. A cycle of acceptable dominance and submission for this couple was wearing thin. This shift paved the way for Mork's acting out in a long-term extramarital involvement with a dependent but controlling woman who Mindy had always detested. What she detested was the influence the woman had on Mork: what salad dressing they should use, what appliances they had to buy, and how to decorate their home. Mork's naïve innocence amused and concerned Mindy. The secretary had more influence over her husband than Mindy had. The spouses had not realized the parallel relational dynamics that the two pairings represented.

Mindy disturbed me too. It was too simple believing Mork was the ill partner and Mindy the long-suffering but healthy partner. A question emerged: Had she married Mork knowing his limitations, and accepted subservience all these years to further their career motives while feigning a loving relationship? The meanings of my hidden digit in the dream did not escape me, although I am embarrassed to admit that the symbol was of the impotence I experienced in the early work with the couple. The hidden digit implied contemptuous feelings for Mork. I wanted to attack his sense of entitlement and his minimizing defenses. He seemed impenetrable, yet I felt penetrated by his aggressive disinterest in much of what I had to say. For example, in one session he got angry and threatened to leave and not return if I continued to bring up unthought aspects of the relationship with the secretary. In fact he referenced his original shock at losing her when he was beginning his career at the early stage of the marriage. I considered that Mindy could be unconsciously splitting off self-loathing into Mork. I might be holding all the negative feelings about Mork in the countertransference in her stead, instead of locating Mindy's contribution to the projective identification.

Mindy had her entitlements. Her career as an administrator in a top architecture firm was problematic. At home, she was used to complete control, disguised as responsibility over the domestic situation, including raising their two daughters (now 23 and 21) while Mork built his career. I thought they shared an unconscious conviction that intimacy was invasion. As long as they unconsciously held to the belief that independence was safer than intimacy, the question of loyalty was unrelated to love. Loyalty was based on specific benefits of monogamy: career building, family, and their mutual enjoyment of golf. Mindy had recently been protesting the "old boy" network at their golf club, in which women were allowed to play together only once per week and early tee times were given to men. Mork protested when Mindy asserted the unfairness. Small chips in the couple's marital container had been increasing lately, as Mork kept his smartphone and e-mail accounts from Mindy's eyes, while Mindy's health had been recently threatened by several bouts with irritable bowel syndrome (IBS). Mork reported cluster headaches starting a few years ago and would not consider extenuating circumstances other than work.

I felt guilty not empathizing with Mork, while slogging my way through what probably coexisted in his unprocessed labyrinth of feelings about women—his wife being one with whom he could not sympathize.

Why did I select Mr. Myogi in my dream? The obvious answer comes from the *Karate Kid* movies in which the calm, containing elderly martial arts sensei takes young Ralph Maccio under his tutelage and turns him from an ineffectual and likable underdog into a champion. His tutelage also gives Maccio the courage to defeat a bully, the rival bad-object sensei's best karate student. Maccio has an Italian last name, so that fits me, but the deeper significance is feeling as the underdog with the couple and needing a sensei to help me regain my senses in working through the negative countertransference with Mork in particular.

Another benefit of a dream while doing couple therapy is the multiple meanings that emerge for understanding both partners. I was made aware of my dyadic "affair" with Mindy as the exciting more accessible partner; I suspect this was an enactment that paralleled Mork's unconscious hunger for the secretary who abandoned him many years ago when he just started his career. In the treatment triangle, I was abandoning Mork for Mindy.

When containment is compromised, dreams, daydreams, and even day-mares can function as a helpful internal supervisor or sensei. The beleaguered container was signified by the small opening early in the dream that I filled with one finger, with no room for expansion; this meant that my container was maxed out—no more room. The end of the dream had a different aspect, illustrating a wish to expand the envelope, at which time Mork appeared sad, as though he knew of my withdrawal and did not want me to give up on reaching him (to him that meant abandonment).

One additional point about containment regarding the unique role of the *patient's unconscious containment of the therapist*: My dream occurred at a crucial point of my feeling hopeless, feeling that I could not treat the couple. This discovery saved the case. When dream material emerges, possibilities are expanded to better understand therapist difficulties or counter-resistances when the therapist dream is about patient containment strategies. Dreams of this sort occur more frequently than is reported in the literature. Patients are in some instances unconsciously containing the therapist's negative feelings in order to provide another chance to create a viable treatment connection.

The field of unconscious communication and the patient's containment of the therapist:

This chapter illustrated an evolution in contemporary psychoanalytic technique previously described by Harold Searles (1975) in detail in "The Patient as Therapist to His Analyst," Steven Cooper (2000) in "Mutual Containment in the Analytic Situation," and Lawrence Brown (2007) on countertransference dreams. I am linking Mork's nonverbal response at the close of the dream to my negative countertransference, and I want us to recognize how Mork sought to modify my rejection of him by titrating (modifying) my anger and neglect of his tortured side. I dreamt of enlarging a space for thinking and in the sequence, Mork responded to a mutual desire for expanding the contact between us and eventually between him and Mindy as well. Detoxifying the harsher aspects of Mork's superego occurred later, as the defensive veneer gave way due to nonsaturating interpretations (here and now transference oriented comments rather than childhood focused). The couple did develop an improved capacity for mutual trust during their three-year treatment by acknowledging and mourning the more malignant projections that kept their marriage in a stalemate.

Chapter Ten

The Couple Therapist's Growth Experience

The in-depth approach to couple therapy is a learning process that inevitably promotes personal and professional growth in the therapist. How does this growth occur? I believe the cognitive and emotional challenges of in-depth work stimulate therapists to confront their personality traits. Therapist narcissism is especially germane when mirroring one's self structure. Being analytically available to unconscious phenomena can bring pleasures and hardships. The couple therapist in self-analysis realizes a distinction between the goals of individual treatment and the goals of couple work: the couple therapists are not preoccupied with pursuing analytic truth, the aim of individual psychoanalysis. Rather, they engage in interactions with a marriage of intimates with two partners bonded but not to the therapist. The feeling of being included and excluded from the couple leads to considerable challenges in the triad. Narcissistic motives can extend to the wish to be within the couple, to be part of the couple, and to exclude a member of the couple due to the therapist's desire to bond in a dyad. These motives come from deep within the therapist's primary object relations and oedipal competitiveness. Countertransference analysis with couples involves a multilayered investigation of the couple as the "patient."

There is a different psychic reality when attending to two individuals in a partnership. Each partner mourns, depends, articulates, feels, and resists in a field in which the nature and meaning of the couple association is the unit of concern.

From the outset I have emphasized the dual importance of learning proper practice theory *and* self-reflection, amplified by the above references. The clinical material in the preceding chapters illustrates the way I practice. In each case the work evolved based on "which" dynamics I selected in order to make therapeutic progress. The readers have had to process the author's rendition of complex communications with his couples and locate themselves in the mix. I ask the reader to test their own clinical situations by trying an experiment with those reported in the book.

The credibility of my couple work ultimately rests on the clinical material and my explanation of what occurred between myself and each couple. Consider your fantasies, associations, and emotional reactions that emerged from chapter to chapter. A personal or subjective experience can stimulate a full exposure of the reader's identifications or counter-identifications with the therapist or the couples presented. In this sense, I invite readers to enter into their subjectivity and embrace whatever occurs—personalize the case material with countertransference feelings, and process the results. This experiment offers a glimpse of the growth available when working in depth because readers will (I hope) derive a deep awareness of their unconscious resonance when affected by the case material. Each therapist works differently and we want to individualize the reader's experience. I offer my experience as an example of working in depth, but offer the caution that way of working is not intended to be replicated in another's practice.

The emotional terrain had to be difficult at times due to the subjectivity inherent in reading about a therapist's and couple's unconscious process. Working in depth is partly a detective story and a mystery in which conceptual mapping is based upon the object relations theory of couple treatment—an intersubjective clinical field. The issue when working in the subjective is that the results are objectively observable, but it is not usually so clear how to get there. Working with unconscious material is about the strange and unfamiliar, and it presses therapists to reach for clinical certainties. The preference for the tangible, more knowable is what has distinguished psychoanalytic work from pragmatic therapies. The reader might be inclined to choose a different path of intervention with these couple cases. The therapist that undertakes a close-up exposure to and confrontation with psychological disturbance must take more risks, given the complex phenomena under study. There is an intertwining of the couple and therapist's internal objects—our personality traits influence their use of us and vice versa.

In each case, we accomplish an understanding of the pathological and normative aspects of mutual influences by applying transference and countertransference ideas. Making proper use of these conceptual tools requires a capacity to endure how we may obscure, become confused, and muck up understanding of the triadic matrix of experience, and hopefully recover by locating personal inconsistencies that determine who is doing what to whom. The dual analysis of us and them is worked on internally and the likelihood is that treatment will be effective due to the deconstruction of projective identifications. Keeping boundaries and the frame intact are accomplished by containing the emotional field, which ensures an individualized approach to each couple.

The dual focus on the therapist's personality and emotional makeup and the way he or she processes a couple's mental space stimulates personal growth in the therapist due to a widening and deepening of emotional resilience. A transformation emerges from comprehending emotional and mental dissonance, thereby sharpening the cognitive mapping of each case and its therapeutic requirements. A clinician's growth is not measured by a faster diagnostic formulation, a smarter assumption of couple dynamics, or decisiveness about what to focus on. It is the other way around. A slow therapeutic pace gathers and transference analysis processes the way one is utilized by the couple, to replicate not-as-yet-known couple objects, so as to gradually allow transference to ripen more fully. Repetition of past object relations (mostly bad objects) leads to recognition of a prior dyadic catastrophe, not yet available for comment. Containment is always partial, as unconscious anxieties and defenses are at work, and we are well advised to hold in mind a partner's or couple's fragility, as they are not yet ready to take in reflective thoughts about their internal disturbances. The capacity to listen patiently for unconscious communication evolves using a mentalizing approach, and that skill set fosters spontaneity in a moment of recognition that defenses are dense in a session and not ready for interpretation; so it makes more sense to acknowledge a partner's anxiousness instead.

Growth is recognized as a "snail's pace" of learning. This type of cognitive/emotional processing informs therapist activity. We wait for a spontaneous opening when playful activity stirs transformative affects during or after a session. Growth in the therapist is verified by the couple's surprised laughter at a moment of irony, when they are less dismissive of what is offered in a session, or when emotional contact is made after many attempts have failed. Growth liberates the couple from terrifying unconscious phantasies by softening the hardened internal events into a symbolic form. Previously the couple externalized internal experiences enacted in their relationships. The childhood demons/fears/paranoid and persecutory elements feel quite real in the adult context. Couples play out in the sessions the worst background situations from each partner's past. Therapy has the effect of translating the fixed ideas in a chewable fashion. The hard food is first metabolized by the therapist who preconsciously and consciously chews and notates dissociated or repressed emotional trauma, deprivations, and neglect as the treatment brings out regressive material. In therapy, history repeats what could not be discerned during childhood and adolescence. Therapist growth and couple improvement are linked, much in the way that parents grow along with their baby when there is attunement.

Growth also comes from recognition of failures, false attempts to hasten change, and hubris. Growth in communication is guided by encountering one's associations, moods, and physical sensations before, during, and between sessions. Couples with a history of physical abuse, for example, can quietly absorb us in parallel feelings of becoming pushed, knocked about, or frightened so that we remain silent for long periods but cannot figure out why.

The utilization of dreams in couple therapy is another source of growth for the therapist. Dreams expand analytic work by bridging past, present, and future and by working through complex couple object relationships in the here-and-now. As the couple therapist becomes more comfortable with reaching for associations, memories and affects associated with internal conflicts, the interpersonal encounter enlivens and enriches the therapeutic instrument of the therapist.

Creativity in therapeutic work involves the discovery of appropriate metaphors and imaginings about the symbolic meanings of couple references, repetitions, and distortions. The couple's story is referenced, and sessions move along, often without acknowledging linkages between the there-and-then with the here-and-now. In some others the therapist's empathic curiosity brings to light what has previously been shadowy and fearful. A connection is made, or a loss is located or revisited that is more integrated than before, as a key affective moment arrives. The story deepens, emotional lifting results, and anxieties once feared and projected into the partner are owned by the self; a freeing of mature relating results; and for the therapist, the transformative activity confirms that therapeutic understanding is being accomplished.

The value and triumph of the therapeutic for the couple that can work through is not the only benefit. We feel the pleasure of deep human contact from what has been shared; the implicit discoveries, not planned for are made possible by our diligence and caring. We strive to be of use to the couple and falter when unable to retain an empathic connection. Like Mr. Myogi in chapter 9, we reached into our vulnerable selves and discovered in the muck and mire of not knowing how to transcend the struggle with the yuckiest of negative countertransference. The ongoing aim was and is to make meaning out of the primitive, by surviving the couple's deepest rages and terrors, by containing that which can make a difference. We find the courage to use what we find in the depth of us—often it is not pretty, but the generative unconscious (Newirth, 2003) provides a better holding and unconscious resonance than it did before because we have absorbed but not been entirely taken over by the couple's ghosts. We can think about them with the couple and raise them from obscurity to consciousness.

Perhaps at the core of the therapist's growth process is the revisiting of childhood or adolescent dreams of unmet or unmetabolized completions within ourselves waiting in the wings stimulated by identifying with various couple situations. Our lost objects are waiting to become found objects (Scharff, 1992), and they foster alertness in difficult moments with troubled couples when we may feel we cannot tolerate them; to be sure there are couples incapable of sustaining a couple therapy experience, no matter how sensitively we engage, due to their fear of being exposed. For those couples with whom we might engage fruitfully, however, if our objects find areas of identification with theirs, the odds of making a difference will improve (though the pathway to locating their convergence may be obtuse, painful, or confusing). We are, after all, particularly sensitized to select among the partner's transferences based on what stirs us. We hope to choose transferences and countertransference reactions to study that promote couple progress. With convoluted or piecemeal discoveries (at a part-object level), we discover important markers of unconscious phantasies, because the couple uses us to help their fragile egos function a bit better; later our efforts can reach a preconscious level of understanding and further our intervention choices. We have faith that something therapeutic will emerge that aids in the couple's adaptive developmental strivings.

The practice of object relations couple therapy hinges on couple therapists' openness to repeatedly discovering their own and the couple's use of mental space. Dealing with the depth of couple disturbance entails the therapist suffering until what lies beneath can be helped to surface and become thinkable. The therapist's empathic curiosity is used so that plumbing unconscious aspects of the couple will be accomplished without doing harm to necessary defenses and so that couples can learn something new while continuing to be who they are. With more disturbed couples, a careful touch is needed when probing defenses against unacknowledged primitive anxiety. At the core of these couple resistances, we notice deep terror against losing one's mind, such as fear of being invaded or destroyed by the therapist's interpretations. Borderline pathology is tricky due to the volatility and oscillation of moods from depressive despair to manic excitement. When encountering a marriage with an obsessional/schizoid partner and a borderline partner, we feel overwhelmed by the individual personality difficulties and wish to escape.

Given the nature of unconscious communication, the holding afforded by our working framework keeps us to the task by maintaining a couple state of mind when pushed and pulled in each partner's direction. We hold to a conviction that one's personal and professional growth derives from processing internal experience of the couple's mental and interpersonal space *in situ*, over and over, and from analyzing transference and countertransference derivatives from sessions while living with uncertainties. When our efforts are successful, frozen affects can be released, projections can be integrated, and lost parts of the partner's wounded past can be recovered and healed. To accomplish these tasks, I have demonstrated how the therapist's use of self is informed and buoyed by object relations practice theory and by the courage to remain open to thinking about and working through confusions, attacks on the frame, and affective discharges. Personal and professional growth is achievable by learning to work from surface to depth.

Chapter Eleven

Are We There Yet?

The Journey and Destination of
Keeping Couples in Treatment

In this final chapter, we review the pathway we have established for the practice of couple therapy and for keeping couples in treatment. The aim of the book was to present material about surface and depth in couple relations and in therapy. We bring together links between effective couple work (destination) and the pathway (method) for getting there. In this chapter, we explore therapist style by juxtaposing countertransference with therapist personal valences, as these connect the pathway to the destination.

To review, the cases offered evidence that difficult couples can be sustained in treatment, but the reader may justifiably feel there is too much to master in learning this approach. Building clinical experience takes time. Learning a treatment for difficult couples requires time and seasoning. Spending hours with couple cases stimulates the reaching for thinking tools, and psychoanalytic concepts are intellectually challenging. We have learned that technique evolves from applying theory to case work, and as we get comfortable, we slowly alter established theory by adjusting technique from couple to couple. Altering technique occurs after observing good and bad effects of our choices with many couples. Many hours of thinking, feeling, and evaluating work in progress are needed on a case-by-case basis to develop confidence in one's judgment.

Complex relational and individual pathologies encountered in practice were represented in the previous chapters, and we placed the reader inside many evocative cases for an experience near exposure to the treatment triad. Each case had its traumas and dramas, and we tested the practice theory chapter by chapter. We encountered regressed couples that some therapists would have divided up into two individual cases, never seeing them together due to the pathologies presented. We encountered couples with problems of divorce, infidelity, narcissism, and parent-child issues, for example, that tested our knowledge and stamina.

Practice theory is the foundation for establishing a pathway to arrive at a clinically effective destination. We test its resuscitative and therapeutic potential session by session. A good theory explains the clinical phenomena encountered in daily work and has efficacy in producing couple-therapist collaboration. Theory in use protects our minds by containing affective flooding to prevent drowning when sitting with the pain-driven chaos of love gone wrong. The reader may have found object relations theory difficult to comprehend due to its terminology. The theory featured in this book makes clinical sense because it illuminates complex unconscious dynamics. Psychoanalytic writers may be more or less clear in expressing their ideas, but they just as easily create ambiguities in the way they interpret concepts and elaborate them to make a point. Authors have the intention to build new ideas from established ones. Various authors expand or shift original meanings, so theory must be placed in a historical context and original terms understood and compared with what came later. There are variations and reworkings of object relations theories, and object relations couple theory is a recent advancement derived from psychoanalysis, neuroscience, attachment theory, systems theory, and chaos theory. Psychoanalytic studies and theory building have expanded from the individual, to families, groups, infant observation, intergenerational transmission of trauma (Scharff and Scharff, 2011), and societal dimensions of unconscious process. Different authors and clinicians selectively employ object relations ideas that make sense to them, preferring to shape and apply those that fit their clinical style. I have been selective with theory based on what fuels my style, organizes the clinical process, and assists with hypotheses I can test out with couples.

Good-enough theory helps build our pathway. It frees the therapist's creative juices to be spontaneous, a not-so-well understood aspect of therapeutic capacity. Rather than viewing spontaneity as a sudden rush of therapist insight craving expression, it involves the coming together of the therapist's sense of deep meaning that lifts understanding in a moment of illumination. The couple is touched by the surfacing of something deeply moving, a gestalt, through the therapist's timely link of past into present, or present into past by introducing a metaphor, analogy, or bit of imagining. A moment of clarity, or perhaps a truth, is reached. Spontaneity can generate a movement into comprehension of buried treasure, such as when missing affect is connected to object hunger (longing for the positive symbiosis with mother) in a case of addictive behavior, or a partner hears for the first time the origins of a shame-based life-long descent into selflessly serving others.

We believe the frame for thinking and guiding therapeutic activity explored in the book is adequate to the task. The therapist can reach the couple and help them with their pain when the setting is safe and trustworthy. This was not accomplished easily. Each case presented specific couple vulnerabilities and levels of mistrust due to specific holding deficits. To structure a proper holding, we individualized treatment by being initially sensitive to anxieties and defenses and waited for an opening in which we could address the couple's pain and anxiety.

No single book can cover the art and skills required for couple work with the breadth and uniqueness of disturbed couples. These book chapters were selected to provide descriptive analysis of specific couple types seen in weekly therapy, and the approaches to each case elaborated the practice approach. Selecting from, rather than rigidly adhering to, an object relations frame has greater potential for success in couple work; a flexible frame prevents rigidity. Optimal therapist qualities essential for working in depth are flexibility, self-reflection, the embracing of surprise, instinct, creativity, a sense of humor, and the finding of opportunities for affective contact. Subjectivity is an important phenomenon of the unconscious field. As stated elsewhere, the reader may be left with important unanswered questions and concerns about how we get from chaos to containment and from conflict to meaningful conversation. Re-reading the case material may assist in locating pivotal moments of contact. The reverse (losing contact) can occur because every session has a life of its own; a hopeful session can precede hopeless one and the other way round.

THOUGHTS ABOUT THERAPIST STYLE AND SUBJECTIVITY

A back-and-forth oscillation will occur between couple and therapist throughout treatment, each individual reaching out to make contact and pulling back when threatened, as in too much stimulating input from the therapist, or a too laid-back style when couples require more engagement. When we embrace the unconscious approach to couple work, we are taking on and influenced by subjective process. We endeavor to understand what helps, and we are apt to study more carefully our mistakes, motivated partly by the guilt associated with failing. Often we must settle for an incomplete explanation due to the subjectivity inherent in human systems. Contact is a result of engaging with the couple's transmission of unconscious disturbances and providing a language for transitioning to meaning-making. Subjective experience implies unconscious-to-unconscious communication. I am reminded of the use of the therapist's dream as but one example of unconscious to unconscious communication. The dream work in chapters 7 and 9 illustrated unique examples of subjectivity in couple therapy. We expanded the field of mental space by an application of couple dreams to treatment. We expanded dream work to couples (and extended to the therapist) and note that psychoanalytic dream work was unnecessarily limited to individuals. Accessing unconscious material from all members in the treatment field promotes therapeutic uses of dreams. A motive for offering my dream was based on an emerging interest in underreporting of the role of containment of the therapist with a couple. I presented my own dream in the case to describe the way the triadic field brings out unconscious material in the therapist crucial for understanding the interpersonal-interpsychic influences of working in depth. In my experience, dream material is underutilized in psychodynamic therapy with individuals, couples, families, and groups and ought to receive more attention in training in the mentioned modalities. I cannot resist one more impassioned argument for expansion of the unconscious field in family and couple therapy in psychotherapy training.

To reiterate, no two sessions are alike; no two therapists work alike. We delved into presenting problems and worked with character traits. The symptomatic behaviors at first observed in the treatment cases were figure and ground. Beginning couple narratives in each case reflected the tip of the psychological iceberg of the couple. Deep wounds and defenses sometimes appeared during the initial exploration of a couple's capacity for utilizing therapy, and, over time, hypotheses amplified and modified initial impressions.

We dealt with hidden anxieties, prior relational failures, and traumatic precursors in each partner's life pressing into the relationship, and, from exploring inner space; we comprehended what type of holding and containment were needed to establish safety and trust. The cases illustrated harder-to-reach couples and threats to establishing a pathway due to long periods of resistance. Couples can remain impervious to what lies beneath concrete presentations for a long time. The ways I reached these couples give a glimpse of my style and use of the frame. I responded to what especially moved me, and my having attended to the things I did also means I ignored other factors; these choices are not always in my awareness. I respond in a moment-to-moment resonance with the flow of couple material, and I strive to be in synch with their issues.

Having presented my version of surface-to-depth couple therapy, I end with some tentative conclusions and caveats. At this juncture, we bring into our discussion another salient element of an effective practice approach. I have touched on therapist personality variables elsewhere. Therapist style is personal and is a unique feature of a treatment. It individualizes treatment by shaping the couple-therapist fit. I continue to marvel at what colleagues say and do with their couples that appears to make a difference, knowing that if it were me doing and saying, I do not think it would be effective. *Know yourself* is one conclusion to be drawn when comparing choices of technique and use of self. Supervision of others has provided a lens into the ways therapists reach their patients. I have learned to respect the work of colleagues that engage differently. When a therapeutic frame is integrated with one's personality I have observed that treatment progresses; there are times that I cannot be sure how it occurred.

Infidelity, divorce, malignant narcissism, and couples with extended kinship disturbances were cases chosen to demonstrate the range of couples seeking therapy. Years of practice have convinced me that what works in one situation or with a particular couple may be the fit between the personalities of the participants and the therapist's comfort level with the couple.

Therapist style can be determined by studying a cross-section of one's cases. We have observed how a particular couple or many couples will bring out or inhibit a therapist's style. In every case, there is a conscious and unconscious matching of personalities, so recognizing one's style and the use of the frame are ongoing requirements of self-study so adjustments will ensure a good fit or the recognition of a poor fit. If the fit is poor and this is recognized at the outset as an impediment to collaboration, it may make sense to refer the couple to a colleague. Self-discipline is needed in monitoring and adapting one's style to the dynamics of couple needs and anxieties and to contain transferences.

Finally, I add to the discussion of therapist style the French analyst Haydee Faimberg's (2005) important conceptual link between the *telescoping of generations* and transference. I apply Faimberg's clinical ideas concerning transgenerational negation of identifications (repressed via trauma), applying her ideas to the disconnections present in couple and family work in which one's history is inaccessible. Unconscious transmission of invisible objects means that our couples cannot access what is contributing to current intimacy conflicts due to alienating identifications. Without transference interpretations and a new language linking present dispositions to past inheritance, the couple is destined to repeat anxieties and self-defeating wish-fulfillment (phantasies). The intergenerational transmission of primary pathological inheritance supports the extension of the treatment to the triad because multiple object relationships broaden and deepen the field for discovering trajectories of unconscious communications. If we accept that past generations of kin are capable of influencing the lives of our treatment couples, we must take into account the ways our past generations affect our perceptions, emotions, and styles. I view therapist style through Faimberg's intergenerational ideas because the internal objects ascribed to our generational pulls unconsciously combine with those of the couple. Multiple transferences and countertransference produce powerful undertows of confusion and distraction. We have enlarged our perspective on the treatment system by conceptualizing transference and countertransference as intergenerational. We conclude that therapist style (and clinical judgment) is influenced by and influences a couple's generational object relations in dynamic relation to the therapist's domain of partially metabolized good, bad, exciting, split-off, and dissociated objects.

When stimulated by couple chaos, if the therapist is robust enough to embrace his multiple internal objects, the potential for comprehending what lies beneath the disturbances in the field improves. My dream in chapter 7 was an example of the surfacing of my internal objects. The dream assisted in freeing up a space for thinking anew about the countertransference. We add the importance of multiple objects to the development of a therapeutic pathway. We monitor the therapist's objects as they range from benign to unmetabolized and notice when they can disturb and resurrect the work. Unconscious internal objects that we monitor are one's marriage or family and (from the distant past) family-of-origin influences, including siblings, extended kin, and ancestors. We include mentors, personal analysts, peers, religious and moral values, and other doctrinaire teachings. Internal object influences can affect perceptions and use of self.

Faimberg (2005) also suggests that the private language of the couple is multidetermined, and our narcissism and preoccupation with internal objects may interfere with listening and discerning what the partners have heard unconsciously; a private language holding family secrets is not easily located. The therapist needs to hear what a partner cannot say, has been forbidden to say, due to suffering from past loyalties that foster denial. Finely attuned therapists are mindful of the unspoken, and they wait for a moment when sufficient silence is available so a partner can fill in the blank or when the therapist can speak from the countertransference and add a missing part of the distant object world. This approach suggests a couple theme can be informed by an intergenerational narrative. Simply put, we supply new meaning or make it possible for the couple to discover it.

I would like to offer an example of therapist valence based on personality to illustrate noncouple induced countertransference: A therapist with an obsessional style focuses on continuities and discontinuities in communication, makes cognitive connections, and can be somewhat emotionally reticent. Couples sitting with this style may view talking as an intellectual activity and get overwhelmed or lost as the therapist puts it all together. The cerebral trumps the visceral, and for some couples there may be a helpless retreat after a brief honeymoon with their brilliant thinker-therapist.

Another style can positively or negatively influence countertransference. The style is of a particularly warm therapist with a soft voice. He or she may find a couple withdrawing into a partially dissociative state and discover an underlying danger associated with nurturing phantasies brought out by the therapist's warm nature. In one case, the wife whose parents labeled her as ignorant as a child (she became a college professor) complained that I spoke too softly and that she could not learn anything from me, while the husband insisted they were getting along better as a result of coming to therapy. I identified with the female partner and felt ignored. To adjust my volume, I would have to shout to reach her. Instead I explored the volume and tone in her memories of the parents' attacks on her mind and asked what happened to her voice at those painful times. It took several attempts to enlarge the field for thinking, but she became aware that she was transferring to me (via projective identification) a voice that no one would hear; hence she was carrying the remnants of the ignored (labeled as "ignorant") child, and I was carrying the object part that represented a child whom no one would hear. She later realized that the defensive aspect of the projection functioned to push away my interest in her thoughts and feelings, as they were too painful. This example instructs that we should not and cannot significantly alter who we are. The fit between our style and personality affects a couple's use of the frame through phantasies—positive or negative. Self-scrutiny helps us recognize and address mild-to-acute reactions partners have to our gender, age, attire, ethnicity, and vocal and nonverbal cues, case by case and session to session.

We do not view these examples as merely good or bad styles; we are examining their contribution to the therapy triad and the ways couples take to them or need for them to be modified depending on differences in personalities and transferences. Style brings out transferences, ranging from idealization to devaluation. These caveats are meant to ground the couple therapist in reflecting regularly on these elements for effective practice—the frame, including its theory base, one's self objects, triadic mental space, unconscious process (including dreams), and of course transference and countertransference.

At this juncture I am interested in the reader's personal experience of couple therapy based on the cases and theory presented. The preceding pages demonstrated analytic sensibility and knowledge that shapes clinical judgment. I believe therapy is effective when couples are moved to renewed hope, at first by developing faith in the therapist, and later by realizing that change is occurring. I believe that for many troubled couples intrapsychic-interpsychic change occurs before improvements become conscious. The lowering of anxiety and defensiveness is transformative, slowly glimpsed as impasses recede because of increased safety. We witness a presence of something new, at first scary as defenses recede—a softening of partner aggression, more openness to listening through gradual internalization of the therapist's careful listening.

Not all couples do well with an object relations approach. Some couples who do not benefit are in a hurry, or display magical beliefs; they demand advice and reject other options, or are not capable of psychological inquiry. They may be psychotic or making haste in burying the relationship and heading for divorce. Those who stay with us for awhile get involved. When we mentalize unconscious process and provide affective resonance, couples start to realize that they matter to us; they begin to make sense of their pain. They eventually matter differently to each other when unconscious object relations histories surface. For therapists willing to learn the modality, the method is there to be tested, modified, and customized.

It is a humbling task when we realize that in-depth treatment takes years to learn. We believe a motivated and well-schooled couple therapist can gradually develop a capacity for working from surface to depth and can keep many couples in treatment. The pathway is rocky, as we have observed, but a therapeutic destination is made possible by attention to detail, the constant loss and renewal of desire to make contact with the partners and their relationship, and when we maintain the courage and curiosity to delve into what lies beneath. We benefit from encountering our own and our couple's mental space and suffer and sacrifice along the way.

At the end of treatment, mourning the couple and the end of treatment needs to be worked through. Objects lost and found includes the found therapist soon to be lost; but, if treatment has been internalized, the therapy relationship continues. We may believe the couple is capable of or could use additional treatment. Partners may need more work, but it is better that they determine when to take their leave. Therapists deal with the loss of a couple privately. To process the experience of found and lost, they may discuss their feelings with trusted colleagues or their partner, in supervision, or in a study group. In evaluating the ending of a couple's therapy, we ask what was accomplished and what we learned, given the issues that we worked on. We pause and consider the couple's capacity for having used treatment and review our capability in treating the relationship. At the close of this book, we continue pondering these questions.

Bibliography

Bader, E., and Pearson, P. (2011). "Facing Our Fears: Why We Avoid Doing Couples Therapy." *Psychotherapy Networker*, blog, The Networker Exchange, NPOO11, November/December.

Bagnini, C. (2000). "The Group Unconscious and the Individual Dream." In J. S. Scharff, and D. E. Scharff (Eds.). *Tuning the Therapeutic instrument: Affective Learning in Psychotherapy* (pp.110–123). Northvale, NJ: Aronson.

———. (2005). "Super-vision or Space Invader? Two's Company and Three Makes for Paranoid Tendencies." In M. Stadter & D. E. Scharff (Eds.). *Dimensions of Psychotherapy, Dimensions of Experience: Time, Space, Number and State of Mind* (pp. 153–164). London: Routledge.

———. (2006). "*Accedere al libirinto dell'inconsio delle coppie attraverso i sogni.*" In G. Tavazza (Ed.). *Interazioni: Clinica e recerca psycoanalitica su individuo–coppia-famiglia* (pp. 45–56). Milano, Italy: Franco Angel.

———. (2003). "The Persecution of Divorce." In J. S. Scharff , and S. Tsigounis (Eds.). *Self-hate in Psychoanalysis.* London: Brunner/Routledge.

Bannister, K., and Pincus, L. (1965). *Shared Phantasy in Marital Problems: Therapy in a Four Person Relationship.* London: Tavistock Institute of Human Relations.

Baranger, M., and Baranger, W. (2008). "The Analytic Situation as a Dynamic Field." In *International Journal of Psychoanalysis*, 89, 795–826.

Barnett, J. (1975). "Narcissism and Dependency in the Obsessional-hysteric Marriage." In *Family Process*, 11, 75–83.

Baum-Baicker, C. (2011). APA Division 39S8 List-Serve: Open Letter Petition to the DSM-5 Task Force. December 12, 2011.

Bion, W. R. (1961). *Experiences in Groups.* London: Tavistock.

———. (1962). *Learning from Experience.* London: Heinemann.

———. (1963). *Elements of Psycho-analysis.* London: Heinemann.

Bollas, C. (1987). *The Shadow of the Object: Psychoanalysis of the Unthought Known.* London: Free Association Books.

Bowlby, J. (1969). *Attachment and Loss: Vol. 1, Attachment.* New York: Basic Books.

———. (1973). *Attachment and Loss: Vol. 2, Separation Anxiety and Anger.* New York: Basic Books.

Britton, R. (1990). *The Oedipus Complex Today: Clinical Implications.* London: Karnac.

Bromberg, P. (1995). "Psychoanalysis, Dissociation, and Personality Organization Reflections." *Psychoanalytic Dialogues*, 5, 511–28.

Brown, L. (2007). "On Dreaming One's Patient: Reflections on an Aspect of Countertransference." In *The Psychoanalytic Quarterly*, 76, vol. 3, 835–861.

Clulow, C. (2006). "Couple Psychotherapy and Attachment Theory." In J. Scharff and D. Scharff (Eds.). *New Paradigms for Treating Relationships.* Lanham, MD: Aronson.

Colman, W. (1993) "Marriage as a Psychological Container." In S. Ruszczynski (Ed.), *Psychotherapy with Couples*, (pp. 70–98). London: Karnac.

Cooper, S. (2000). "Mutual Containment in the Analytic Dialogue." *Psychoanalytic Dialogues,* 10, 169–94.

Dicks, H. V. (1967). *Marital Tensions: Clinical Studies towards a Psycho-analytic Theory of Interaction.* London: Routledge.

Faimberg, H. (2005). *The Telescoping of Generations: Listening to the Narcissistic Links between Generations.* London: Routledge.

Fairbairn, W. R. D. (1952). *Psychoanalytic Studies of Personality.* London: Routledge.

Fisher, J. V. (2005). *The Uninvited Guest: Emerging from Narcissism towards Marriage.* London: Karnac Books.

Fosshage, J. L. (1983). "The Psychological Function of Dreams." *Psychoanalysis and Contemporary Thought*, 6, 641–69.

Freud, S. (1900). *The Interpretation of Dreams.* SE Vol. VII.

———. (1914). *On Narcissism*, SE, Vol. XIV.

———. (1917). "Mourning and Melancholia." *Standard Edition* 14, 243–58.

———. (1933). *New Introductory Lectures in Psychoanalysis.* SE, Vol. XXII.

Glickauf-Hughes, C., & Wells, M. (1995). *Treatment of the Masochistic Personality.* Northvale, NJ: Aronson.

Greenberg, J., & Mitchell, S. (1983). "W. R. D. Fairbairn." In *Object Relations in Psychoanalytic Theory* (pp.151–187). Cambridge MA: Harvard University Press.

Grotstein, J. S. (2007). "The Container and the Contained." In *A Beam of Intense Darkness: Wilfred Bion's Legacy to Psychoanalysis* (pp. 151–168). London: Karnac.

Guntrip, H. (1961). *Personality Structure and Human Interaction: The Developing Synthesis of Psychodynamic Theory.* London: Hogarth Press.

Gurman, A. S., & Jacobson, N. S., (2002). *Clinical Handbook of Couple Therapy.* 3rd Edition. New York: The Guilford Press.

Holmes, J. (2001). *The Search for a Secure Base: Attachment Theory and Psychotherapy.* New York: Taylor & Francis.

Klein, M. (1935/1975). "A Contribution to the Genesis of Manic Depressive States." In *Love, Guilt and Reparation and Other Works, 1921–1945* (pp. 344–369). London: Hogarth Press.

———. (1946). "Notes on Some Schizoid Mechanisms," In *International Journal of Psychoanalysis*, 27, 99–110.

———. (1948). *Contributions to Psycho-analysis, 1921–1945.* London: Hogarth Press.

———. (1952). "The Origins of Transference." In *Envy and Gratitude and Other Works: The Writings of Melanie Klein*, Vol. III. London. Hogarth Press.

Lachkar, J. (1992). *The Narcissistic/Borderline Couple: A Psychoanalytic Perspective on Marital Treatment.* New York: Brunner/Mazel.

Martin, E., and Schurtman, R. (1985). "Termination Anxiety as It Affects the Therapist." *Psychotherapy*, 22, 92–96.

McCormack, C. (2000). *Treating Borderline States in Marriage.* Northvale, NJ: Aronson.

Meltzer, D. (1967). *The Psycho-analytical Process.* London: William Heinemann Medical Books.

Morgan, M. (1995). "The Projective Gridlock: A Form of Projective Identification in Couple Relationships." In S. Ruszczynski and J. Fisher (Eds.). *Intrusiveness and Intimacy in the Couple* (pp. 33–48). London: Karnac.

Newirth, J. (2003). *Between Cognition and Emotion: The Generative Unconscious.* New York: Other Press.

Ogden, T. H. (1982). *Projective Identification and Psychotherapeutic Technique.* New York: Aronson.

Perelberg, R. J. (2009). "Murdered Father; Dead Father: Revisiting the Oedipus Complex." *International Journal of Psychoanalysis*, 90, 713–732.

Pittman, F. (1990). *Private Lies: Infidelity and the Betrayal of Intimacy.* New York: Norton.

Ruszczynski, S. (Ed.). (1993). *Psychotherapy with Couples: Theory and Practice at the Tavistock Institute of Marital Studies.* London: Karnac Books.

Ruszcynski, S. and Fisher, J. (Eds.). (1995). *Intrusiveness and Intimacy in the Couple.* London: Karnac Books.

Scharff, J. S., and Bagnini, C. (2001). "Object Relations Couple Therapy." In A. S. Gurman, and N. S. Jacobson (Eds.), *Clinical Handbook of Couple Therapy* (3rd Edition) (pp. 59–85). New York: Guilford Press.

———. (2004). "Narcissistic Disorder." In D. Snyder, and M. Wisman (Eds.), *Treating Difficult Couples* (pp. 285–307) New York: Guilford Press.

Scharff, D. E. (1992). *Re-finding the Object and Reclaiming the Self.* Northvale, NJ: Aronson.

Scharff, D. E., and Scharff, J. S. (1987). *Object Relations Family Therapy.* Northvale, NJ: Aronson.

———. (1991). *Object Relations Couple Therapy.* Northvale, NJ: Aronson.

————. (2000). *Tuning the Therapeutic Instrument :Affective Learning in Psychotherapy*. Northvale, N.J.: Aronson.

————. (2011). *The Interpersonal Unconscious*. Northvale, NJ: Aronson.

Schecter, D. E. (1979). "The Loving and Persecuting Superego." Presidential Address. William Alanson White Psychoanalytic Society, New York, May 23, 1979.

Searles, H. (1975). "The Patient as Therapist to His Analyst." In P. Giovacchini (Ed.), *Tactics and Techniques in Psychoanalytic Therapy: Vol. II Countertransference* (pp. 95–151). New York: Aronson.

Segal, H., and Bell, D. (1991). "The Theory of Narcissism in the Work of Freud and Klein." In J. Sandler et al. (Eds.), *Freud's "On Narcissism: An Introduction"* (pp. 149–174). New Haven, CT: Yale University Press.

Siegel, J. (1992). *Repairing Intimacy: An Object Relations Approach to Couples Therapy*. Northvale, NJ: Aronson.

Slipp, S. (1984). *Object Relations: A Dynamic Bridge between Individual and Family Treatment*. New York: Aronson.

Solomon, M. F. (1989). *Narcissism and Intimacy: Love and Marriage in an Age of Confusion*. New York: Norton.

Stern, D. N. (1985). *The Interpersonal World of the Infant: A View from Psychoanalytic and Developmental Psychology*. New York: Basic Books.

Suttie, I. (1935). *The Origins of Love and Hate*. Middlesex, England: Penguin Books.

Tuber, S. (2008). "The Meaning and Power of Play." In *Attachment, Play, and Authenticity: A Winnicott Primer* (pp.119–137). Lanham: Aronson.

Whitman, R. M., Kramer, M., Baldridge, B. J. (1969). "Dreams about the Patient—An Approach to the Problem of Countertransference." *Journal of the American Psychoanalytic Association*, 17, 702–727.

Winnicott, D. W. (1956). "Primary Maternal Preoccupation." In *Through Paediatrics to Psycho-analysis: Collected Papers* (pp. 300–305). New York: Brunner-Mazel.

————. (1971). *Playing and Reality*. London: Tavistock.

————. (1986). "Children Learning." In C. Winnicott et al. (Eds.), *Home Is Where We Start From: Essays By a Psychoanalyst.* (pp. 143–149). Norton: New York.

Index

adhesive bond, ix
affair: session illustrating confession of an, 104; background to session illustrating confession of an, 104–105. *See also* infidelity
affect. *See* dream interpretation; dreams
alpha functioning, 153
analytic third, 45, 87
antilibidinal object (Fairbairn), 94
assessment, 34–36; object relations initial couple assessment, 36. *See also* narcissism; narcissists
attachment styles, ix
attunement, xv, xvii, 24, 68, 149–150

Bader, E., xviii
Bagnini, Carl, ix, 23, 28–29, 36, 122
Bagnini, Susan, xxiv
Bannister, K., 23
Baranger, M., 23
Baranger, W., 23
Barnett, J., 28
Baum-Baicker, Cindy, 7
Bion, Wilfred R., 23, 31, 45, 76, 149
blocking, 54
Bollas, Christopher J., 22, 152
borderline-schizoid marriages, 60
Bowlby, John, 24
Britton, Ronald, xix, 30
Brown, Lawrence, 163

"C" (rejection of curiosity) defenses, 76
claustrum, 159
Clulow, Chris, xix
cognitive-behavioral therapy, 5, 7, 9–10
Coleman, W., xix
collusion as a dynamic in treatment, 94
containment/containing, 149–151; in a couple case, 155–163; defined, 3, 150; features of, 153–154; masculine and feminine symbols and, 151–152; mutual, 152; patient's unconscious containment of therapist, 162; separate sessions within couple treatment, 154–155; strains on, 96–97
contextual transference, 129, 149
Cooper, Steven H., 163
countertransference, xvi, xxi, 30, 179–181; defined, xvi; divorce and, 145–147; to dreams, 119–121; non-couple-induced, 181. *See also* couple therapists
couple matrix, 7.4.. *See also* dreams; projective matrix
couple state of mind, 31
couple therapists: expectations and assumptions of well-meaning, 71–73; underlying process of expectations and assumptions of well-meaning, 74–76; growth experience of, 165–171; self-awareness of, xvi; style and subjectivity of, 176–183

About the Author

Carl Bagnini, LCSW, BCD is a founding senior faculty of the International Psychotherapy Institute and former National Chair of the Object Relations Child, Couple, and Family Therapy Training Program of IPI. He is on the faculties of the Adelphi University Gordon Derner postgraduate programs in clinical supervision and couple and marital therapy, and the New York Institute for Psychotherapy Training. Carl has published and coauthored many book chapters and papers on individual, couple, and family therapy, supervision, and related clinical topics. He has practiced and taught for more than forty years, and has been a featured presenter at major conferences in the United States, Europe, and Panama. He regularly presents by video-conferencing and on Skype. His clinical practice is in Port Washington, New York.

CPSIA information can be obtained at www.ICGtesting.com
Printed in the USA
BVOW070757300512

291167BV00002B/2/P